SOUTHEASTERN COMMUNITY COLLEGE
NEW DIRECTIONS FOR TEACHING AND LEARNING

Marilla D. Svinicki, *University of Texas, Austin*
EDITOR-IN-CHIEF

Teaching and Learning on the Edge of the Millennium: Building on What We Have Learned

Marilla D. Svinicki
University of Texas, Austin

EDITOR

D1519100

Number 80, Winter 1999

JOSSEY-BASS PUBLISHERS
San Francisco

TEACHING AND LEARNING ON THE EDGE OF THE MILLENNIUM: BUILDING ON
WHAT WE HAVE LEARNED
Marilla D. Svinicki (ed.)
New Directions for Teaching and Learning, no. 80
Marilla D. Svinicki, Editor-in-Chief

ISSN 0271-0633   ISBN 0-7879-4874-8

NEW DIRECTIONS FOR TEACHING AND LEARNING is part of The Jossey-Bass
Higher and Adult Education Series and is published quarterly by Jossey-
Bass Inc., Publishers, 350 Sansome Street, San Francisco, California
94104-1342. Periodicals postage paid at San Francisco, California, and at
additional mailing offices. Postmaster: Send address changes to New
Directions for Teaching and Learning, Jossey-Bass Inc., Publishers, 350
Sansome Street, San Francisco, California 94104-1342.

New Directions for Teaching and Learning is indexed in College Student
Personnel Abstracts, Contents Pages in Education, and Current Index to
Journals in Education (ERIC).

SUBSCRIPTIONS cost $58.00 for individuals and $104.00 for institutions,
agencies, and libraries. Prices subject to change.

EDITORIAL CORRESPONDENCE should be sent to the editor-in-chief, Marilla
D. Svinicki, The Center for Teaching Effectiveness, University of Texas at
Austin, Main Building 2200, Austin, TX 78712-1111.

Cover photograph by Richard Blair/Color & Light © 1990.

www.josseybass.com

Printed in the United States of America on acid-free recycled paper containing 100 percent recovered waste paper, of which at least 20 percent is
postconsumer waste.

Contents

About This Publication. Since 1980, *New Directions for Teaching and Learning (NDTL)* has brought a unique blend of theory, research, and practice to leaders in postsecondary education. *NDTL* sourcebooks strive not only for solid substance but also for timeliness, compactness, and accessibility.

The series has four goals: to inform readers about current and future directions in teaching and learning in postsecondary education, to illuminate the context that shapes these new directions, to illustrate these new directions through examples from real settings, and to propose ways in which these new directions can be incorporated into still other settings.

This publication reflects the view that teaching deserves respect as a high form of scholarship. We believe that significant scholarship is conducted not only by researchers who report results of empirical investigations but also by practitioners who share disciplined reflections about teaching. Contributors to *NDTL* approach questions of teaching and learning as seriously as they approach substantive questions in their own disciplines, and they deal not only with pedagogical issues but also with the intellectual and social context in which these issues arise. Authors deal on the one hand with theory and research and on the other with practice, and they translate from research and theory to practice and back again.

About This Volume. In this issue, we take time to reflect on the progress that has been made in the field of teaching and learning since the first issue of *New Directions for Teaching and Learning* was published some twenty years ago, including discussions of some of the most popular issue topics. We also speculate on the directions the series will take in the next twenty years.

MARILLA D. SVINICKI, editor-in-chief, is director of the Center for Teaching Effectiveness at the University of Texas, Austin.

EDITOR'S NOTES

When Bob Menges called me back in 1990 to invite me to work with him on editing *New Directions for Teaching and Learning,* I didn't even let him finish his prepared speech before jumping at the chance. I had long viewed this series as one of the most influential and useful publications in the field of college teaching and learning. The chance to have some input into its development was too great to resist. Working with Bob on the series has been the most professionally rewarding experience of my career in faculty development.

This issue is both a marker of the millennium and an anniversary issue celebrating *NDTL*'s twentieth year. Before his untimely death in 1998, Bob and I had conceived of this "millennium issue" as an opportunity to reflect on what the series had accomplished, how the field had changed, and where we were headed in the next century. We asked the people at Jossey-Bass to help us choose the chapter topics by providing a list of the best-selling issues over the life of the series. Excluding topics for which we had issues in the works, we selected the six featured in Part Two for showcasing in this celebratory volume.

We invited editors of the original issues to return to their topics and reflect on what has happened in those areas in the interim. In all cases, the topics have not only continued to be of critical interest to the field but have developed into substantial movements within higher education pedagogy—witness the explosion of group work, critical thinking, and technology in teaching, for example. And the field itself has grown, as evidenced by the plethora of new information resources available.

The other component of this issue was to be a review of the foundation of *New Directions for Teaching and Learning:* research informing practice. The two cornerstones that inform our practice are research on learning and motivation and research on teaching itself. The result is the two chapters in Part One discussing how far that research has come since *NDTL* began. One of the key goals of this series has been to provide practitioners with current theory and research findings that can be coupled with practical applications. Its aim has been to be the first stopping place for faculty seeking new ideas about teaching and learning. All the editors of *NDTL* worked with that as a central purpose—with admirable success.

Finally, we wanted to point to the future. Where is higher education going in the twenty-first century? A final chapter on future trends, in Part Three, offers some things to think about in that regard.

Preparing this issue has been a wonderful experience for me. It makes me grateful all over again to Bob Menges for allowing me to participate in creating this most important resource. Even though he is no longer a phone call away when tricky editorial questions arise, Bob continues to help us make those decisions by the standards he set when we worked together. He would have every reason to be proud of the series to this point; we hope to continue to honor his vision as we move into our next decade and a new century.

Marilla D. Svinicki
Editor

MARILLA D. SVINICKI is editor-in-chief of the New Directions for Teaching and Learning series and is director of the Center for Teaching Effectiveness and senior lecturer in the Department of Educational Psychology at the University of Texas at Austin.

PART ONE

Theory and Research on Learning and Teaching

1

Half of the mandate for New Directions for Teaching and Learning *is to monitor developments in learning theory and research. This chapter discusses the changes in learning and motivation theory that have influenced the field since the beginning of the series.*

New Directions in Learning and Motivation

Marilla D. Svinicki

At the time of the inaugural issue of *New Directions for Teaching and Learning* in 1980, psychological research and theory in the area of learning and motivation were about to undergo a sea change, one that would have important implications for the design of instruction. The shift was from a behavioral perspective on learning to a cognitive perspective and its successors in constructivist and personal responsibility models of learning. The purpose of this chapter is to discuss each of these models in turn and the instructional paradigms that were based on them. We have not abandoned earlier instructional methods as new theories have come along, but we have realigned some of our interpretations of what is going on when learning takes place.

The Behaviorist Model

In the 1960s and early 1970s, the behaviorist model had become the dominant model in psychology (Greeno, Collins, and Resnick, 1996). According to that model, learning was the development of associations between stimuli and responses or stimuli and other stimuli through the act of pairing and the delivery of contingencies based on responses. Behaviorism was a very important movement for psychology at the time, even though it had rejected much of the work that had gone before it as unscientific. The reasoning was that in order for psychology to be a science, it had to focus on repeatable, verifiable, observable events that everyone could agree had taken place. There was no advantage to resorting to nonobservable mediating events like thinking because environmental consequences were capable of explaining even very complex chains of behavior (Skinner, 1953).

Though the model may seem a bit drastic in retrospect, it was an important step in psychology's attempt to be accepted as a science. Adopting the scientific criteria of observation and replication meant that psychology was trying to move away from speculative and mysterious causes of behavior into a more positivist approach that identified verifiable cause-and-effect relationships.

Instructional Implications. During its tenure as the dominant theory, behaviorism provided a lot of good information and ideas about the causes of learning. The purpose of instruction under behavioral models was to increase the frequency of correct responses and minimize errors. Learners were fairly passive participants in the whole process. They merely responded and experienced the consequences of the response. Positive consequences increased the response's probability; negative consequences decreased it. The instructor organized the learning environment to ensure that correct responses were likely to occur, and when they did, they were rewarded. Incorrect responses were either punished or ignored and as a result lost strength.

Perhaps the most prominent and long-lasting instructional method that came from the behaviorist tradition was self-paced instruction. A typical self-paced instruction course has the following components that derive from behaviorist traditions:

The outcome is specified in clear, observable terms known as behavioral objectives. Still in use today in the somewhat modified form of instructional objectives, the goal of behavioral objectives was to identify the actual behavior that the learner would be able to display at the end of instruction, the conditions under which it would be displayed, and the criteria that would determine acceptable performance. This was clearly an outgrowth of the behaviorists' desire for reliable measures of behavior that could be observed objectively. The existence of such objectives went a long way toward persuading educators to be clearer in their goals and outcome measures, a noble goal regardless of one's theoretical background. (For more details on objectives, see Mager, 1962.)

The target behaviors were divided into small, easy-to-achieve steps presented in a logical sequence that would build toward the final complete behavior. Such a careful sequencing of behavior components required that the final task be analyzed into its components and each component taught to mastery before going on to the higher-level components, another useful concept.

The mastery criterion for moving on was an important part of self-paced instruction and its counterpart, mastery learning. Mastery learning itself was shown to be the form of group learning that came closest to the results of individual tutoring (Bloom, 1984).

From this practice came the idea of criterion-referenced evaluation of learning. Rather than compare students with one another to determine progress, students were measured against their own progress toward specified criteria.

Students receive immediate feedback on the correctness of their response. A critical component of behavior theory was the contingent and proximal relationship between the learner's response and its consequences. In some self-paced methods, such as programmed texts, the learning materials themselves were designed to provide immediate feedback to the learner.

Although behavior theory itself might be out of vogue, self-paced instruction and its derivatives live on in several guises. The most obvious is computer-assisted instruction. One of the reasons that programmed instruction texts never quite made it big in education was their tediousness, forcing every student through the same sequence regardless of performance or purpose. Some textbook authors tried to incorporate a form of individualization into the text by using branching, in which one's next step in the book is determined by one's answer to the previous step. This was a much better system from the learner's perspective, but the intricacies of developing such printed materials were viewed with disfavor by publishers.

Enter the computer, which is able to handle branching with ease. In fact, although hypertext was actually derived from a different theory of psychology, the support programs it spawned allowed computer-assisted instruction to pick up where programmed instruction left off and successfully implement self-pacing on a large scale. Successful computer-assisted instruction incorporates virtually all of the values of self-paced instruction along with some new wrinkles that allow the program to be even more tailored to the individual user (Cognitive and Technology Group at Vanderbilt, 1996).

Behavior theory also suggested the concept of hierarchical sequencing of behaviors and the value of teaching components in a particular order. This strategy involved analyzing the components of the final behavior and having the learner master each one in order as a way of achieving the target behavior. Robert Gagné (1965) expanded on this idea with his concept of systematic instructional design based on a hierarchy of behavior types. He also proposed that each different type of learning target would require a different type of instruction. Although Gagné's model does not adhere strictly to a lot of the tenets of behavior theory, it does have a strong behaviorist slant and has been quite influential in educational design.

Today the predominant use of behaviorist recommendations is in the area of class organization and management (Chance, 1999). The specification of course objectives helps both learner and instructor understand the target behaviors or level of understanding being sought in a course. The concept of criterion-referenced grading, basing the grade on the level achieved rather than the comparison with other students, is strongly encouraged as a way of minimizing the detrimental effects of competition and encouraging the beneficial effects of cooperation. The concepts of reinforcement, punishment, and extinction are still very valuable in thinking about ways to encourage and discourage behavior. As a heuristic for making management decisions in class design, behavior theory has served us well.

However, behavior theory has not been as helpful in advising instructors about how to structure the actual teaching material. Aside from the concepts of task analysis and small steps carefully sequenced, behavior theory does not speak directly to the design of instruction. And it ignores the one thing we most equate with learning: thinking. As educators and learners ourselves, we know that the bulk of what is happening in education is the restructuring of thinking and understanding, and about those behavior theory was relatively mute. However, along with the rest of psychology, behavior theory eventually came to the conclusion that much of the behavior we see really was based on internal mediation, that is, thinking. Part of this conversion of behavior theory and the rest of psychology was a result of the next wave of theories, known as cognitive theories (Pressley and McCormick, 1995).

The Cognitive Model

In the 1970s and 1980s, the ideas of cognitive psychology began to resurface in the field. The initial versions of cognitive theory were still fairly mechanistic and continued to revolve around the concept of associations among stimuli, but now the focus was on mental associations, which could only be inferred from external responses made by the learner (Anderson, 1983). Learners were still somewhat at the mercy of environmental input, but at this point, the influence of the learner began to be considered. This influence was primarily a result of the effects of the learner's prior knowledge and existing schemata (concepts) on the storage and organization of new information, so it was not as if the learner was actively directing his or her learning yet. Storage of new information in memory could still theoretically occur without active direction by the learner. In a fairly simplistic way, incoming information could bounce around in the learner's consciousness until it was matched with the same or a similar pattern already stored in memory, at which point the memory pattern was either strengthened or modified to accommodate the new information.

These early cognitive theories focused on learning as a structuring and restructuring of memory. Information coming in from the environment received the learner's attention and as a result entered consciousness (working memory), where it was held briefly until either processed into long-term memory, discarded as unimportant, or displaced by incoming information. These theories, called information processing theories, were most useful in advising teachers how to design instruction that would benefit this form of learning; they were not very useful in classroom or behavior management.

Instructional Implications. The goal of instruction under this paradigm is to organize the presentation of new information so that it can be easily stored in memory. To maximize learning, the instruction needs to focus learner attention on the critical features of information; provide supports for using storage strategies, such as analogies, examples, clear definitions, and well-organized presentations; and incorporate opportunities for learners to respond, on the basis of their understanding of material, in order to determine if it had been correctly stored. One can see that under this system, the learner's preexisting storage system (prior knowledge) would have a strong impact on how new information would be stored. An inaccurate or inefficient filing system in long-term memory would seriously hamper information retrieval, so it was important to get it right the first time or to ferret out misconceptions (inaccurately filed information) (Chi, Slotta, and De Leeuw, 1994; McCloskey, 1983).

Let us look at some of the instructional strategies that derive from early cognitive theory.

Strategies for Directing Student Attention to Key Points. These include highlighting of main ideas in information presentations, either verbally ("the next main idea is . . .") or visually with bold print, underlining, and italics in text material or visual aids in oral material.

Strategies for Emphasizing How Material Is Organized. These include outlines, concept maps, flow diagrams, analogies, advance organizers (given before the information is presented), tables, comparative charts, and verbal cues that signal structure, such as "I have three main points" or "Now let's consider the other side of the argument." It is also useful to have the learners articulate the organization of the material for themselves by drawing their own concept maps, outlines, or analogies.

Strategies for Making Information More Meaningful for the Learner. Because cognitive theory is based on the idea of mental associations and a network structure to long-term memory, it holds that the more associations a learner can make between new and old information, the easier retrieval will be. To facilitate this, the instructor can activate the learners' prior associations by asking the learners to think about what they already know, using examples that are within the ken of the learners and might be part of their personal experiences, asking the learners to supply examples of the concept being learned, giving vivid or richly detailed descriptions of instances of the concept, and giving multiple examples of the concept in a variety of contexts.

A variant on this meaningful learning recommendation is the related issue of understanding the learner's prior knowledge before starting instruction (Alexander, Kulikowich, and Schulze, 1994; Ausubel, Novak, and Hanesian, 1978). As noted earlier, the learner's existing long-term memory structures could either support or hinder new learning. In the first case, the instructor would be able to build on preexisting structures and take advantage of the rich information base the learner already has, if the teacher knows what that is. In the latter case, the instructor could confront misconceptions early in learning so that they don't get in the way.

An interesting sidelight about how this particular aspect of cognitive theory has made its way into instructional practice is the advent of hypertext and hypermedia. This contemporary instructional concept is directly related to the way cognitive theory proposes that long-term memory is structured

(Bakker and Yabu, 1994). We think of long-term memory as a network of associations, some well organized and some unique. This is translated into the network structure of hypertext. Concepts are linked to one another, some in well-organized ways and other in unique ways. Hypermedia was intended to mimic the way we actually think: through associations that are often idiosyncratic, based on our experiences, but logical nevertheless. This connection between computer hypermedia use and cognitive theories of learning has led to a great deal of interesting research and product development. For example, one very common problem in hypermedia environments is the phenomenon of getting lost in the network and being unable to reproduce the thinking that got one there. Theoretically, this could be a result of not having a "big picture" of the overall structure of the content area. Researchers are now suggesting that having access to a concept map of the overall database, known as a site map, with one's current position highlighted (a sort of "you are here" aid) and one's path marked, could keep learners from getting lost in hyperspace (Bakker and Yabu, 1994).

Strategies for Encouraging Active Checking of Understanding. Most of the instructional strategies that encourage active learning derive from the value of retrieving information from long-term storage early enough in learning to monitor how it is being stored and correct any errors before they become too deeply ingrained. These include asking frequent questions during the presentation of material, having students explain their understanding to other students (the think-pair-share model), and using classroom assessment techniques (Angelo and Cross, 1993) like minute papers. From a motivational standpoint, these activities also provide an opportunity for learners to get feedback on their understanding.

Strategies That Recognize the Limitations of the Learning System. One aspect of the cognitive model that has not yet been mentioned is the proposed limited capacity of working memory and the implications for instruction. Although long-term memory is theoretically unlimited and permanent, working memory storage is very temporary. What we are conscious of at the moment is what is present in working memory. Our ability to cope with the immediate demands of the environment is circumscribed; we can attend to only a part of what is going on around us. The now famous "seven plus or minus two bits of information" dictum even quantifies exactly how much (or little) we can remember for a short period of time (Miller, 1956).

There are all kinds of implications of this limited capacity. For example, a continuous stream of new information with no breaks cannot be processed rapidly enough by most learners. Therefore, lecturers need to attend to the density of information they are delivering if they want the learners to do more than simply write down everything they say. Actually stopping talking for a while after giving a very important piece of information is a recommendation. Another way to provide a break without actually stopping is to repeat or rephrase the point just made. No new information is coming in, so the learner is able to digest what is being said more readily.

The same effect can be accomplished by giving examples: no new information, just an elaboration on the existing point.

Another implication of the capacity of working memory is that when multiple demands are being made on the learner, capacity is being divided up among them, thus leaving less for each. We can see this whenever we are going to hand back an exam at the end of class. The students spend the whole class dividing their attention between what we're saying and worrying about the exam. The latter steals capacity away from the former, and there is no way to combat it effectively (Ormrod, 1999). Not even giving back the exams at the beginning of class will do it: in that case, students' attention shifts from worrying about the exam to trying to figure out what they did wrong. This same mechanism is postulated as one of the bases for the effects of test anxiety. Instead of being able to devote their entire working memory capacity to answering test questions, test-anxious students have part of that capacity taken up by worry over how they're doing. Anything that increases that worry will cause more attentional capacity to be occupied unproductively. As a result, programs that treat test anxiety are often focused on helping the learner focus less on worry and more on the test itself.

The Cognitive Model, Phase II: Metacognition

The model just described was extremely useful in making recommendations about the way to structure learning materials and situations to maximize understanding, but it was not totally satisfactory. There were still unexplained results and a feeling of dissatisfaction with the role of the learner (or the lack of a role) in the learning process. Identical instruction provided to two different learners with similar experience and background still couldn't produce the same learning with 100 percent certainty. Something was missing from the equation. That something was the full participation of the learner. Granted that cognitive theory took into account prior knowledge and individual differences in processing capacity, but the learner could still be a fairly passive respondent under the original models. What was missing was active learner involvement at all levels of processing. Thinking of ourselves as passive learners doesn't fit with our personal experiences. We believe that we are in charge and actively directing the course of learning. This belief led to the next phase of cognitive theory, one in which the learner is aware of learning and actively directing it. The process was named *metacognition*, or "thinking about thinking" (Brown, 1978).

Although the learning processes of storage and retrieval are still the same, in metacognition the learner is involved in directing that process. Current theory proposes that we are learning for a purpose, to achieve a goal we have set, and we are aware of that goal, using it throughout the learning process to assess progress. To achieve the goal, we have analyzed the requirements of the task, our skills, and alternative strategies (if we have any) for moving toward the goal. We have selected one alternative for any number of reasons (some good, some not so good) and implemented it. Now we begin to monitor our comprehension and progress. If we start to go astray, we back up and reassess our strategies for learning. Is a different strategy called for at this point, or is it just a matter of more effort? Through this continuous cycle, we progress toward the goal and eventually achieve it.

As one can see, this is a much more learner-centered, learner-directed interpretation of learning and motivation than either the behaviorist model or the initial cognitivist model.

Instructional Implications. Most of the instructional implications that were true in the original cognitive model remain true under metacognition. The difference is in who is responsible for invoking them. In the original version of cognition, the *instructor* was the director of the process; with metacognition, that responsibility is turned over to the *learner* with support from the instructor. Unfortunately, many, if not most, learners are not particularly metacognitively aware. They have often mastered only one or two strategies for learning, strategies that are fairly applicable but not universal. They may have adopted inappropriate criteria for deciding whether or not they have learned and as a result stop too soon or fail to recognize an inappropriate strategy until they get independent feedback from the outside, usually in the form of a failed exam. In the face of such negative feedback, they don't know what to do or they react in emotionally inappropriate ways that limit their ability to correct their errors. So the advent of the concept of metacognition meant that instructors needed to raise student awareness of themselves as learners and sometimes even teach them how to learn.

Let us examine some instructional strategies that derive from the concept of metacognition.

The instructor should model thinking. Skills are often best taught through a type of apprenticeship. In this case, that apprenticeship revolves around metacognition: it is a *cognitive apprenticeship.* Instructors can demonstrate how they monitor and direct their own learning by thinking aloud while solving problems in front of the class. Following this with a discussion about the kinds of strategies the instructor invoked will give learners a model to copy in their own thinking (Collins, Brown, and Newman, 1989).

Instructional methods should support metacognition. Instructional methods such as writing journals, describing problem solutions in prose as well as mathematical format, and discussing problem-solving strategies in a group context are all ways of encouraging students' metacognitive growth. Metacognition, like any other skill, requires practice opportunities, so an instructor should build these into the regular activities of the class (Collins, Brown, and Newman, 1989).

Sometimes direct teaching of strategies is needed. As noted earlier, some students have limited strategies for problem solving. Especially if they are studying in a content area outside their own field, they may not be aware of what kinds of strategies are possible. Even brief demonstrations of alternatives or written suggestions about strategies to use can alert students to the fact that there is more than one way to solve a problem and teach them new strategies, a method called *supplemental instruction* (Martin and Arendale, 1994). Granted, most students when they are under pressure revert to old strategies, but with additional practice, they may at least come to understand the value of trying different methods (Pressley and others, 1989).

The Cognitive Model, Phase III: Learner-Centered Models

Since the mid-1980s, there has been a subtle shift in learning and motivation theory toward the concept of learner-centeredness, including constructivist theory in epistemology (Fosnot, 1996), self-regulation in learning control (Pintrich, 1995), and self-determination in motivation (Deci, Vallerand, Pelletier, and Ryan, 1991), which mirrors a larger social shift toward personal responsibility. Metacognition was the first wave of theorizing to promote the idea that the learner had to be driving the process of learning. Since then, more and more attention has been paid to active control by the learner and the motivational value of that control. Also known as *strategic learning*, the concept of a learner who sets goals, marshals resources, makes strategic decisions about resource use, and evaluates the entire process in an ongoing manner seems a better fit for our own experiences and those reported in the literature (Weinstein, 1996).

In fact, some theorists have proposed various versions of *constructivism* to emphasize the degree to which learners are constructing their own worldview. These theories lie on a continuum from the simple influence of prior knowledge on the understanding of new information to the idea of knowledge existing only in and drawing on the context of the learning situation, an idea called *distributed cognition* (Bereiter, 1990). Here the basis for understanding by learners involves not just their own prior knowledge and present experience but that of other individuals who are interacting with them in the situation, as well as the situation itself. These are the concepts of social constructivism (Bruner, 1990) and situated cognition (Brown, Collins, and Duguid, 1989), respectively.

Constructivism and social constructivism form some of the foundation for collaborative learning strategies that are gaining popularity (Hertz-Lazarowitz, Kirkus, and Miller, 1991). These theories assert that learning is the process of developing a *construction* of reality in the mind of the learner. Through interactions with the environment and interpretations of those interactions, the learner comes to create a worldview consistent with past experience and present data. Collaboration among learners is a very potent way in which an individual learner forms an interpretation of the environment and develops understanding. Some constructivists believe that this understanding is an accurate reflection of an external reality, while others hold that one cannot really talk about an objective reality because all understanding is filtered through the perceptions of the learner. Despite these divergent views, constructivism has been the basis of many of the most recent instructional innovations, particularly collaborative learning.

The concept of situated cognition (sometimes called *situative learning* in the literature [Greeno, Collins, and Resnick, 1996]) actually has a long history behind it even though it has only recently been named. In the past, what we now refer to as situated cognition was played out as issues of transfer of learning. In fact, it was the difficulty of getting students to transfer what they had learned in one setting to a new setting that started psychology down the path toward situated cognition. There was quite a lot of controversy about whether there were general rules of thinking and problem solving or only content-specific rules (Perkins and Salomon, 1989). Although the argument is too complex to discuss here, one of the main points was that it might be that some of the cues needed to solve a problem existed only in the context of that problem itself—in other words, the solution was *situated* in the context (Resnick, Levine, and Teasley, 1991). When one attempted to remove the solution from the context and apply it elsewhere, those cues were no longer available, and therefore the solution would no longer work unless one could find analogous cues in the new situation (Greeno, Collins, and Resnick, 1996). Such a proposition obviously has tremendous implications for instruction.

Instructional Implications. With the advent of learner-centered theories of learning and motivation have come some new instructional methods.

Strategic Learning and Self-Regulation. As outlined in the previous discussion, the first of these methods is the idea of strategic learning (Weinstein, 1996) and self-regulation (Pintrich, 1995). Instructors can create opportunities for students to learn and exert self-regulation of their learning by involving the students in setting learning goals, in selecting and implementing learning strategies, and in monitoring their own learning.

Learning in Groups. Even beyond the teaching of learning strategies, today's instructors are encouraged to offer the learner more opportunities to make decisions about what and how to learn, if not individually, then at least as part of a collaborative group. Learners and instructors become partners in a learning community. The most recent instructional innovations in collaborative learning (Brown and Palincsar, 1989) and communities of learners (Brown and Campione, 1994; MacGregor, Cooper, and Smith, in press) have their roots in this shift toward increased individual control over learning, strange as that may seem. This is one justification for collaborative learning structures. In working with others to understand material, the learners have more open access to their own understanding and thinking processes (Johnson and others, 1981). They get more immediate and more personal feedback to assist in the monitoring process. And they have more of a sense of personal control and ownership of the material and thus more motivation

(Deci, Vallerand, Pelletier, and Ryan, 1991). They are also motivated by participating in a community of practice (Lave and Wegner, 1991).

Authentic Problem Solving. Instruction should be based on authentic problem-solving tasks. From the standpoint of situated cognition and improving the potential for transfer of learning, several new instructional methods have been developed. All depend on creating learning environments that are as close to the real environment of practice as possible. By reproducing or involving the learner in "legitimate peripheral participation" (Lave and Wegner, 1991) in the actual functions of the discipline, the instruction provides both the situational cues for responding and the motivation for putting forth the effort.

The methods that are still classroom-based, which simulate the problem-solving process of field professionals, are quite diverse in implementation but common in purpose and process. For example, problem-based learning (Wilkerson and Gijselaers, 1996) and discovery learning (Bruner, 1991) both require learners to solve problems that are similar in nature and complexity to the real thing. For problem-based learning, this might be a medical problem; for discovery learning, it might be a natural phenomenon to investigate. In some cases, such as in anchored instruction (Cognition and Technology Group at Vanderbilt, 1990), the problems are lengthy and multifaceted and involve numerous domains of skills and knowledge for solution. In the terms of the theorists, the instruction is *anchored* in a very complex and realistic task. With the advent of multimedia, it has become possible to present learners with very complex problems and very realistic environments even in the context of the classroom.

In both discovery-based and problem-based learning, the focus is on the process of problem solving rather than the solution itself. Learners, usually working in groups, determine the questions to ask, the methods to gather data, and the ways to interpret the data obtained. More important, they are asked to reflect on their own problem-solving process in an effort to increase their awareness of it.

Taking the situations a step further toward situated learning, some instructors are moving students out of the classroom and into authentic learning settings. This has long been the case in some disciplines, as evidenced by laboratory or fieldwork and clinical placements. Those tended to be fairly specific to the sciences in the case of the former and professions in the case of the latter. Now, however, more general educational goals are being pursued in programs like service learning (Rhoads and Howard, 1998). In these forms of instruction, the instructor often becomes less of a master and more of a co-learner.

Cognitive Apprenticeship. Instruction can take advantage of the concept of learning by observing an expert model. An interesting blend of old instruction and new is the discussion of the *cognitive apprenticeship* (Collins, Brown, and Newman, 1989). In the past, skills were learned by working in an apprenticeship relationship with a master craftsman who explained the craft while demonstrating it and involving the learner with slowly increasing responsibility. Collins, Brown, and Newman (1989) suggest that a similar instructional process can be used for cognitive skills. Here the learner (the apprentice) would observe the instructor (the master craftsman) go about the business of thinking about the field while describing the thought processes aloud. The instructor gradually places more and more responsibility for problem solution on learners until eventually the learners can solve the problems on their own. During this transition, the instructor supports the learners' efforts, coaches them with questions and suggestions, and encourages them to think aloud about their solution processes. Collins and colleagues provide several examples of how this is done in different educational settings.

The Unique Learner

Another area of research on learning that warrants discussion is the role of individual differences among learners and the contributions those differences make to learning and motivation (Corno and Snow, 1986). Attempts to categorize learners by ability levels or learning styles for the purpose of simplifying the design of instruction (for example, "all visual learners benefit from pictures") have resulted in less than convincing data or in burgeoning subcategories as more and more differences among learners appear with further study (Jonassen and Grabowski, 1993). In the end, we must acknowledge that human learning is the product of so many different variables—some of which can be measured, most of which cannot—that our efforts to simplify it are doomed from the start. The best we can hope to do is list some small portion of those variables that have been studied scientifically and design sufficient variety into our instruction that most learners will find something to meet their needs. At the same time, we can equip learners with a range of experiences and learning strategies so that they become self-regulated learners as discussed earlier and therefore capable of adapting to any style of instruction.

What are some of the learner variables that we can consider? Here are just a few of the most frequently mentioned ones.

Level of prior knowledge. If there is one thing that all psychologists can agree on, it is that the level of prior knowledge that the learner brings to the situation is the biggest individual variable in determining how much is learned. There is not much an instructor can do to guarantee homogeneous backgrounds among the learners, but the instructor can certainly make an attempt to find out what the range is and offer remediation for students whose backgrounds are below standard (Bransford and Johnson, 1972; Anderson and Pearson, 1984; Chi, Glaser, and Farr, 1988).

Cognitive processing variables. Learners process information in many ways. For example, some learners prefer to take their learning in a series of logical steps from beginning to end, building to a conclusion (serial learners); others prefer to begin their learning with an overview, the "big picture," and then fill in with the details later (holistic learners) (Entwhistle, 1981). It is probably more efficient to offer an overview initially and then provide the details, because this strategy will benefit the most students and has other advantages from a cognitive processing standpoint.

Personality variables. Some theorists include personality variables in the list of individual differences. For example, some learners can look at a whole picture and isolate or abstract individual pieces with ease (field-independent learners); others are strongly influenced by the whole picture and do most of their interpreting of new information in the context in which it occurs (field-sensitive learners) (Witkin and Goodenough, 1981). Abstraction is easier for the former type of learners, and integration is probably easier for the latter. An instructor can include both types of tasks in learning so as to benefit those students when their preference is being matched and to help them learn to adjust to task challenges that do not match their preferences.

Another personality variable is that learners may be impulsive or reflective (Schmeck, 1988b), tending to respond either quickly or more thoughtfully. This dichotomy is sometimes interpreted as risk-taking versus cautious learning. Whatever its underlying mechanism, this variable can have an influence on students' responsiveness in class, on their test-taking behavior, and even on their choice of assignments.

Strategies for learning. Recent theorists have proposed the concept of *learning strategies* as an area of individual difference (Weinstein and Meyer, 1986). These strategies are learned rather than part of a learner's basic personality structure. They include such techniques as creating visual images to assist with memory, relating new information to already learned information, and organizing information into an easily remembered outline structure. Students show a preference for different types of strategies based on their past experiences. For example, some students use surface strategies that concentrate primarily on memorization or the identification of surface features to aid in retention. Other students look beyond the surface features and try to understand the underlying structure of information; they are called deep processors. Many systems of learning strategies have been studied (Entwhistle, 1987; Marton and Säljö, 1976; Weinstein and Meyer, 1986; Weinstein, Goetz, and Alexander, 1988; Schmeck, 1988a), and each system makes a valuable contribution to our understanding of how students invest their time during learning.

Beliefs about learning and thinking. Student beliefs about knowledge and what it means to understand contribute to the individual variability we see in the effects of teaching (Wigfield, Eccles, and Pintrich, 1996; Hofer and Pintrich, 1997; Halpern, 1998). Students who believe that knowledge is a resource provided by an authority will have a very different approach to learning and goals from a student who believes he can create his own understanding. This is a particularly interesting perspective on how different learners might be influenced in their approaches to learning. In addition, it has been suggested that students need to have a disposition toward problem solving, a tolerance for ambiguity, and several other qualities to work successfully at some of the higher cognitive levels.

Demographics. Variables such as age, gender, and ethnic background each contribute some special qualities to learners (Pascarella and Terenzini, 1991; Baxter-Magolda, 1992; Anderson and Adams, 1992). This has been an area of great interest, but not a source of much usable advice for faculty.

Many areas of difference have been proposed as having an influence on learning. In reality, many of these tendencies are simply the result of preferences or experiences rather than some inborn trait of the individual. A good example is the proposed difference between auditory, visual, and kinesthetic learners (Dunn, Beaudry, and Klavas, 1989). This particular system for classifying learners is very strongly ingrained in our experience. I have even been known to use it myself (Svinicki and Dixon, 1987). But evidence that it is anything but a preference remains to be gathered. As a preference, this distinction does have a useful role to play in the design of instruction, but it does not explain the why behind the preference.

Another fairly commonly held belief about learning is that each individual has his or her own learning style and that attempts to circumvent that style will be thwarted because their basis is deeply grounded in the individual's psyche. The concept of learning style, however, is a slippery one and not as strongly supported in the literature as one might think (Jonassen and Grabowski, 1993). Each "style" inventory reflects an underlying model of learning, which is often not articulated for the user. Theories that attempt to simplify or classify individuals into a small number of "types" do an injustice to the complexity of human behavior. Even in the individual differences discussed in this chapter, the range of individual response is so great and the overlap so encompassing that I hesitate to support any system that seeks to classify people. Perhaps the most egregious error along these lines is the belief that if we can identify a person's type, we know all we need to know about that person, as if naming were the same thing as explaining—or the belief that "once a Type A, always a Type A," as if behavior were driven by some basic individual force that cannot be modified. Neither of these assertions is justified, at least at this point in the growth of the field (Jonassen and Grabowski, 1993).

The same cautions should be exercised when talking about the current "brain-based learning" methods. Although physiological psychology is making huge strides in its ability to study the brain processes, it is nowhere near being able to explain behavior on the basis of which area of the brain is being used. Rather, the more research is done, the more it appears that each hemisphere of the brain is being used in most activities. Therefore, it is inappropriate or at least premature to speak of a person as "left-brained" simply because he or she shows a preference for logical analysis over holistic analysis. Such claims, and the accompanying instructional methods they purport to underlie, should be viewed with caution and skepticism at this point.

Instructional Implications. The crux of this discussion is that it is appropriate to acknowledge that there are individual variables among students that can influence the effectiveness of instruction. However, more research is needed to verify which of the proposed differences is most strongly grounded in empirical data and has the best record of relating to learning. Until those data have been gathered and properly analyzed, our best instructional strategy to cope with individual differences is to provide an array of learning alternatives and let the learner choose among them rather than trying to force one on everyone or even on a single individual.

Motivation from a Learning Perspective: The Answer to Everything?

I teach students who aspire to be teachers at a variety of levels from preschool to college level, and I find that they all have inordinate faith in the ability of motivation to overcome all obstacles. I don't share their confidence in motivation; after all, no matter how motivated I am to be as good a tennis player as Martina Hingis, I'll never reach that goal owing to age and lack of physical prowess. But I understand how potent a force motivation can be and how much face validity it has for teachers and learners alike. For that reason, it has been the subject of an entire *New Directions* issue (Theall, 1999). Even though we've touched on it at several earlier points in the chapter and its relation to teaching will be illustrated more thoroughly in Chapter Two, I will review a few of the more standard theories of motivation from the perspective of the learner rather than the instructor.

Theories of motivation have followed the same sequence as theories of learning in terms of their conceptual basis. They have evolved from a behavioral perspective to a cognitive perspective and beyond. For a really complete summary of theory, I recommend Theall (1999) or Pintrich and Schunk (1996). See Table 2.1 in Chapter Two as well.

Behavior Theory and Motivation. Motivation had a peculiarly unique status in early behaviorist traditions. In essence, it didn't exist. Because behaviorists originally believed that behavior was caused solely by past contingencies, motivation, which implied a looking ahead or anticipation of future consequences, couldn't really exist. A learner engaged in a behavior not in anticipation of being reinforced when he finished but rather because that behavior had been reinforced in the past. Modern versions of behaviorism include a concept of the incentive value of future rewards or anticipated consequences as a factor in influencing the occurrence of a response.

What behaviorist theory did contribute, however unintentionally, to motivation was the concepts of reinforcement and punishment as drivers of behavior. As noted earlier, reinforcement is a very useful construct for teaching. We should provide positive consequences when students engage in a desired behavior. If we do, that behavior is more likely to occur again in the future. Likewise, we should provide negative consequences when students engage in undesirable behavior, which will lower its frequency. This is a perfectly legitimate way to think about classroom management, and most instructors naturally use these strategies all the time.

Under the *cognitive paradigm,* motivation for learning was thought of primarily in terms of the need to have consistent, accurate, and useful understandings of the world. Learners were motivated to learn when feedback on their responses indicated a mismatch between their memory structure and the "real world." If learners made a choice based on their associations or their understanding of how the world worked and that choice produced negative feedback (by turning out to be wrong), they were motivated to seek more information and to change either the response or the underlying association.

Of course, there is a whole array of theories that speculate on why negative feedback would be so motivating. For example, self-worth theory maintains that individuals respond in a way that will maintain their image of self-worth (Covington, 1984). One possible response to information that they have made a mistake (and therefore might experience reduced self-worth) is to figure out what went wrong and correct it. Other ways to respond to mistakes are to deny that the initial response was wrong, to try to find some mitigating circumstance that caused the wrong response but still preserves self-worth, or to blame someone or something else for the mistake—all popular student responses to negative feedback and ones we would like to discourage.

Motivation in other versions of the cognitive model is based on how learners think about the consequences of their behavior. Here theory emphasizes learner goals, expectations, and beliefs—in short, cognitions. A particularly useful motivation theory along these lines is called expectancy-value theory (Atkinson and Birch, 1978; Eccles, 1983). In this theory, a learner's motivation is a function of how likely success at a task is (expectancy) and the value the learner places on that task (value). Both components must be present in some degree for the learner to be motivated. Instructors can intervene to help raise student expectancy for success or to increase the value of the task for that learner.

Expectancy for success is also discussed as *self-efficacy* in many theories (Bandura, 1989). The concept of self-efficacy is a belief in one's own ability with regard to a specific task. Learners with high self-efficacy for test taking believe in their general ability to cope with test-taking situations. However, self-efficacy can be destroyed if learners experience a disconnection between their behavior and its consequences. When learners have this kind of experience, they often exhibit what is called *learned helplessness*, a general low level of motivation attributed to the belief that nothing they could do will make a difference (Seligman, 1975). This condition and its associated symptoms of lethargy, passivity, and dependence are frequently seen in students.

Goals and their impact on learning are another cognitive motivational concept that is very useful (Schunk and Zimmerman, 1994). In this version of the theory, student motivation is tied to progress toward a goal in several ways. First, the difference between current level of performance and the goal is thought of as a source of motivation. Learners will work to narrow that gap. And when students see they are making progress toward the goal, they will be more motivated to continue. Finally, when students see that others who have reached the goal receive positive benefits, they develop an anticipation that if they, too, reach the goal, they will receive those same benefits.

Another particularly useful cognitive theory is attribution theory (Weiner, 1980) and its offspring, explanatory style (Peterson and Seligman, 1984), in which learners' motivation is based on what they believe causes their success or failure. For example, if they attribute success to luck rather than ability, they are not as motivated, because luck is hard to predict. If they attribute failures to outside forces, they may also be unmotivated, for they have no control over those forces. In general, attribution theories recommend focusing learners' attention on things over which they have some reasonable control and accepting the fact that sometimes one has no control over the outcome.

One recent addition to the cognitive models of motivation has been goal orientation theory (Ames, 1992; Dweck, 1986). In this theory, the learner's behavior is determined to a great degree by the type of goal for learning. The two major goal orientations are mastery goal orientation and performance goal orientation. Students with a mastery goal orientation are motivated by the desire to learn something new. They are not concerned with how long it takes or how many mistakes they have to make to learn. Students with a performance goal orientation are motivated by the desire to demonstrate existing competence, especially in comparison with peers. One might think of these two orientations as related to Eison's learning orientation/grade orientation model (1981). The latter model would be a natural extension of the former.

One can imagine the differences in overt behavior under these two orientations (Ormrod, 1999). A mastery orientation tolerates risk-taking; performance doesn't. Mastery seeks corrective feedback; performance wants only confirmatory feedback. Mastery views mistakes as learning opportunities; performance views them as evidence of failure. This particular model has many implications for working with students and their goals, as we shall see.

With the advent of more models based on personal control concepts, motivation theory has also moved in that direction. One recent manifestation of that move is self-determination theory (Deci, Vallerand, Pelletier, and

Ryan, 1991). In this theory, motivation is based on the learner's perceptions of being in control of his or her own destiny. In self-determination theory, the greatest motivation is felt when learners makes their own choices about how to learn or what direction to take. Also connected to self-determination theory is the attributional concept of belief in an internal control over outcomes, known as locus of control (Weiner, 1986). When learners have choices and believe that their success rides on those choices, they are highly motivated to put forth effort.

A very familiar topic in motivation is the issue of intrinsic versus extrinsic sources of motivation. Intrinsic sources are those that arise from engaging in the task itself, whereas extrinsic sources come from outside the learners. Current theory and research have concluded that the best sources of motivation are those that are intrinsic (Deci, Vallerand, Pelletier, and Ryan, 1991; Ames and Ames, 1991; Csikszentmihalyi, 1975). Intrinsic motivation comes from having choices, from choosing challenging yet attainable goals, from feelings of being in control, and from self-efficacy for the task at hand. The combination of choice, challenge, and competence is proposed as the best situation for fostering intrinsic motivation.

A new concept in motivation is the idea of volition. If motivation is the force that gets a behavior started, volition is the force that keeps it going in the face of obstacles (Corno, 1993). Volition involves using strategies that help the learners overcome obstacles, cope with frustration, and carry the task through when completion seems far away. We can see lack of volition strategies in the tendency of some students to give up if they can't solve a problem immediately. One possible way to improve student motivational strategies is to teach them how to carry through as well as how to get started.

Instructional Implications of Motivation. Each motivation theory offers slightly different recommendations for teachers, but all are useful in thinking about how to create a learning environment that is motivating for the learners. The following are some of the instructional strategies that derive from the various theories discussed.

Provide reinforcement for activities you wish to encourage. Praise, positive feedback, points, or access to highly desirable activities (like not having to take a final) all can be used to reinforce students for participating in class or completing work as scheduled. The advantage of using positive consequences such as praise is that it has a net positive effect on the class atmosphere, which then contributes to better learning itself.

Emphasize internal reinforcers and motivation. Giving students choices about what they will do or organizing learning around existing student interests is a way of tapping into internal motivation with the advantage that the activities become self-reinforcing and the teacher's role is minimized.

Set challenging yet attainable goals for learning, and provide feedback on progress. Note the emphasis on attainable goals. Students need to believe that they have a chance of meeting expectations. The goals cannot be so simple that they are meaningless, but they should also not be beyond the capacity of the learners. In addition, involving the learners in setting their own goals is a useful enhancement to this recommendation. The opportunity to set one's own goals is motivating and gives the learner more of a vested interest in their attainment.

Change learner beliefs and attitudes about learning. In terms of motivation, several theories revolve around learners' beliefs and attitudes. To increase motivation, instructors are advised to help learners develop appropriate attributions about what causes their successes or failures. Most research points to encouraging students to make the connection between effort and success. If the learners believe that effort is responsible for their successes, they will be more willing to work hard and persist in the face of difficulties.

Encourage a mastery goal orientation. From a motivational perspective, instructors are advised to help students adopt a mastery orientation to their work. There are many suggestions for doing so, but most involve removing or minimizing student-to-student comparisons that we so often make and focusing more on self-comparison or comparison with the end goal.

Enhance the perceived value of the task. Expectancy-value theory recommends helping students understand the value of a learning task. This can be done by making the task more challenging or more interesting, by showing the utility of the skills to be learned, or by showing how the task matches the goals of the learner.

Convince the learners they can succeed; increase their self-efficacy. The other half of the expectancy-value theory is about raising student expectations about their own capacities to succeed. Instructors can help learners believe that they can accomplish the target task by pointing out the correspondence between already established skills and the new task, by giving the learners some early successes, by verbally supporting their effort—anything that will bolster their self-confidence.

Give the learner choices about goals and strategies for achieving them. Although it is not always possible to achieve the ideal of self-determination, instructors can give students choices over how they will pursue a fixed goal ("use whatever works for you as long as you learn this week's vocabulary") or choices over which goal to pursue using a fixed procedure ("write a research paper, create a display, or give a presentation on the topic of your choice using a particular information searching model").

Conclusion

It is impossible in the confines of this publication to discuss all the research on learning that has influenced instructional design over the past twenty years. What is presented here merely skims the surface. The theories and recommendations continue to evolve even as I write these words.

If I had to summarize what the research and theory on learning and motivation have to say to teachers at the turn of the twenty-first century, it would be that more than ever we believe that learners are at the center of the teaching and learning process. As teachers, we can filter, highlight, guide, give feedback, and encourage, but the biggest variable in what determines final performance is what the learners bring to the table. The learners' prior knowledge and its structure, their learning strategies, goals, beliefs, self-efficacy, and motivations all contribute to their learning. This view is complex, but there is no cause for despair. Although we as instructors may have less personal influence on learning than we thought, we certainly know more about the process of learning, and that is suggesting a lot of ways to support learning.

What may be the biggest development in learning for higher education is the simple fact that we are now starting to pay attention to it at all. Researchers are making progress in identifying variables that affect learning, instructors are recognizing that knowing about learning can significantly improve teaching, and students are becoming more informed about alternative ways to improve their own learning. As theories of learning, bolstered by better research, are giving us more accurate descriptions of learning and predictions of its outcomes, we are moving toward a more unified vision of what needs to be done to make learning happen.

References

Alexander, P., Kulikowich, J. M., and Schulze, S. K. "How Subject-Matter Knowledge Affects Recall and Interest." *American Educational Research Journal*, 1994, *31*, 313–337.

Ames, C. "Achievement Goals and the Classroom Motivational Climate." In D. H. Schunk and J. Meece (eds.), *Student Perceptions in the Classroom*. Mahwah, N.J.: Erlbaum, 1992.

Ames, R., and Ames, C. "Motivation and Effective Teaching." In R. Idol and B. Jones, *Educational Values and Cognitive Instruction*. Mahwah, N.J.: Erlbaum, 1991.

Anderson, J. A., and Adams, M. "Acknowledging the Learning Styles of Diverse Student Populations: Implications for Instructional Design." In L.L.B. Border and N. V. Chism (eds.), *Teaching for Diversity*. New Directions for Teaching and Learning, no. 49. San Francisco: Jossey-Bass, 1992.

Anderson, J. R. *The Architecture of Cognition*. Cambridge, Mass.: Harvard University Press, 1983.

Anderson, R. C., and Pearson, P. D. "A Schema-Theoretic View of Basic Processes in Reading." In P. D. Pearson (ed.), *Handbook of Reading Research*. New York: Longman, 1984.

Angelo, T. A., and Cross, K. P. *Classroom Assessment Techniques: A Handbook for College Teachers*. (2nd ed.) San Francisco: Jossey-Bass, 1993.

Atkinson, J. W., and Birch, D. *Introduction to Motivation*. (2nd ed.) New York: Van Nostrand, 1978.

Ausubel, D. P., Novak, J. D., and Hanesian, H. *Educational Psychology: A Cognitive View*. (2nd ed.) Austin, Tex.: Holt, Rinehart and Winston, 1978.

Bakker, P. A., and Yabu, J. K. "Hypermedia as an Instructional Resource." In D. F. Halpern and Associates, *Changing College Classrooms: New Teaching and Learning Strategies for an Increasingly Complex World*. San Francisco: Jossey-Bass, 1994.

Bandura, A. "Human Agency in Social Cognitive Theory." *American Psychologist*, 1989, *46*, 157–162.

Baxter-Magolda, M. B. *Knowing and Reasoning in College: Gender-Related Patterns in Students' Intellectual Development*. San Francisco: Jossey-Bass, 1992.

Bereiter, C. "Aspects of an Educational Learning Theory." *Review of Educational Research,* 1990, *60,* 603–624.

Bloom, B. S. "The Search for Methods of Group Instruction as Effective as One-to-One Tutoring." *Educational Leadership,* 1984, *41,* 4–17.

Bransford, J., and Johnson, M. K. "Contextual Prerequisites for Understanding: Some Investigations of Comprehension and Recall." *Journal of Verbal Learning and Verbal Behavior,* 1972, *11,* 717–726.

Brown, A. L. "Knowing When, Where, and How to Remember: A Problem of Metacognition." In R. Glaser (ed.), *Advances in Instructional Psychology,* Vol. 1. Mahwah, N.J.: Erlbaum, 1978.

Brown, A. L., and Campione, J. "Guided Discovery in a Community of Learners." In K. McGilly (ed.), *Classroom Lessons: Integrating Cognitive Theory and Classroom Practice.* Cambridge, Mass.: MIT Press/Bradford, 1994.

Brown, A. L., and Palincsar, A. S. "Guided, Cooperative Learning and Individual Knowledge Acquisition." In L. Resnick (ed.), *Knowing, Learning, and Instruction: Essays in Honor of Robert Glaser.* Mahwah, N.J.: Erlbaum, 1989.

Brown, J. S., Collins, A., and Duguid, P. "Situated Cognition and the Culture of Learning." *Educational Researcher,* 1989, *81,* 32–42.

Bruner, J. *Acts of Meaning.* Cambridge, Mass.: Harvard University Press, 1990.

Bruner, J. "The Act of Discovery." *Harvard Educational Review,* 1991, *31,* 21–32.

Chance, P. *Learning and Behavior.* (4th ed.) Pacific Grove, Calif.: Brooks/Cole, 1999.

Chi, J., Glaser, R., and Farr, M. (eds.). *The Nature of Expertise.* Mahwah, N.J.: Erlbaum, 1988.

Chi, M., Slotta, J., and De Leeuw, N. "From Things to Processes: A Theory of Conceptual Change for Learning Science Concepts." *Learning and Instruction,* 1994, *4,* 27–43.

Cognition and Technology Group at Vanderbilt. "Anchored Instruction and Its Relationship to Situated Cognition." *Educational Researcher,* 1990, *19,* 2–10.

Cognitive and Technology Group at Vanderbilt. "Looking at Technology in Context: A Framework for Understanding Technology and Education Research." In D. C. Berliner and R. C. Calfee (eds.), *Handbook of Educational Psychology.* New York: Macmillan, 1996.

Collins, A., Brown, J. S., and Newman, S. E. "Cognitive Apprenticeship: Teaching the Crafts of Reading, Writing, and Mathematics." In L. Resnick (ed.), *Knowing, Learning, and Instruction: Essays in Honor of Robert Glaser.* Mahwah, N.J.: Erlbaum, 1989.

Corno, L. "The Best-Laid Plans: Modern Conceptions of Volition and Educational Research." *Educational Researcher,* 1993, *22,* 14–22.

Corno, L., and Snow, R. "Adapting Teaching to Individual Differences Among Learners." In M. Wittrock (ed.), *The Handbook of Research on Teaching.* New York: Macmillan, 1986.

Covington, M. "The Motive for Self-Worth." In R. Ames and C. Ames (eds.), *Research on Motivation in Education,* Vol. 1. Orlando, Fla.: Academic Press, 1984.

Csikszentmihalyi, M. *Beyond Boredom and Anxiety.* San Francisco, Jossey-Bass, 1975.

Deci, E. L., Vallerand, R. J., Pelletier, L. G., and Ryan, R. M. "Motivation and Education: The Self-Determination Perspective." *Educational Psychologist,* 1991, *26*(3–4), 325–346.

Dunn, R., Beaudry, J., and Klavas, A. "Survey of Research on Learning Styles." *Educational Leadership,* 1989, *46,* 50–58.

Dweck, C. S. "Motivational Processes Affecting Learning." *American Psychologist,* 1986, *41,* 1040–1048.

Eccles, J. "Expectancies, Values, and Academic Behaviors." In J. T. Spence (ed.), *Achievement and Achievement Motivation.* New York: Freeman, 1983.

Eison, J. "A New Instrument for Assessing Students' Orientation Towards Grades and Learning." *Psychological Report,* 1981, *48,* 919–924.

Entwhistle, N. J. *Styles of Learning and Teaching.* Chichester, England: Wiley, 1981.

Entwhistle, N. J. "Explaining Individual Differences in School Learning." In E. De Corte, H. Lodewijks, R. Parmentier, and P. Span (eds.), *Learning and Instruction: European*

Research in an International Context, Vol. 1. Leuven, Belgium: University of Leuven Press, 1987.

Fosnot, C. T. (ed.). *Constructivism: Theory, Perspectives, and Practice.* New York: Teachers College, 1996.

Gagné, R. M. *The Conditions of Learning.* Austin, Tex.: Holt, Rinehart and Winston, 1965.

Greeno, J., Collins, A., and Resnick, L. "Cognition and Learning." In D.C. Berliner and R. C. Calfee (eds.), *Handbook of Educational Psychology.* New York: Macmillan, 1996.

Halpern, D. F. "Teaching Critical Thinking for Transfer Across Domains: Disposition, Skills, Structure Training, and Metacognitive Monitoring." *American Psychologist,* 1998, *53,* 449–455.

Hertz-Lazarowitz, R., Kirkus, V. B., and Miller, N. "An Overview of the Theoretical Anatomy of Cooperation in the Classroom." In R. Hertz-Lazarowitz and N. Miller (eds.), *Interaction in Cooperative Groups.* New York: Cambridge University Press, 1991.

Hofer, B., and Pintrich, P. R. "The Development of Epistemological Theories: Beliefs About Knowledge and Knowing and Their Relation to Learning." *Review of Educational Research,* 1997, *67,* 88–140.

Johnson, D. W., and others. "Effects of Cooperative, Competitive, and Individualistic Goal Structures on Achievement: A Meta-Analysis." *Psychological Bulletin,* 1981, *89,* 47–62.

Jonassen, D. H., and Grabowski, B. L. *Handbook of Individual Differences, Learning, and Instruction.* Mahwah, N.J.: Erlbaum, 1993.

Lave, J., and Wegner, E. *Situated Learning: Legitimate Peripheral Participation.* New York: Cambridge University Press, 1991.

MacGregor, J., Cooper, J., and Smith, K. (eds). *New Directions for Teaching and Learning,* no. 81. San Francisco: Jossey-Bass, in press.

Mager, R. *Preparing Instructional Objectives.* (2nd ed.) Belmont, Calif.: Lake, 1962.

Martin, D. C., and Arendale, D. R. (eds.). *Supplemental Instruction: Increasing Achievement and Retention.* New Directions for Teaching and Learning, no. 60. San Francisco: Jossey-Bass, 1994.

Marton, F., and Säljö, R. "On Qualitative Differences in Learning. I: Outcomes and Process." *British Journal of Educational Psychology,* 1976, *46,* 4–11.

McCloskey, M. "Naive Theories of Motion." In D. Gentner and A. Stevens (eds.), *Mental Models.* Mahwah, N.J.: Erlbaum, 1983.

Miller, G. A. "The Magic Number Seven, Plus or Minus Two: Some Limits on Our Capacity for Processing Information." *Psychological Review,* 1956, *63,* 81–97.

Ormrod, J. *Human Learning.* (3rd ed.) Upper Saddle River, N.J.: Prentice Hall, 1999.

Pascarella, E. T., and Terenzini, P. T. *How College Affects Students: Findings and Insights from Twenty Years of Research.* San Francisco: Jossey-Bass, 1991.

Perkins, D., and Salomon, G. "Are Cognitive Skills Context-Bound?" *Educational Researcher,* 1989, *18,* 16–25.

Peterson, C., and Seligman, M. "Causal Explanations as a Risk Factor for Depression: Theory and Evidence." *Psychological Review,* 1984, *91,* 347–374.

Pintrich, P. R. (ed.). *Understanding Self-Regulated Learning.* New Directions for Teaching and Learning, no. 63. San Francisco: Jossey-Bass, 1995.

Pintrich, P. R., and Schunk, D. H. *Motivation in Education: Theory, Research, and Application.* Upper Saddle River, N.J.: Merrill, 1996.

Pressley, M., Goodchild, F., Fleet, J., Zajchowski, R., and Evans, E. D. "The Challenges of Classroom Strategy Instruction." *Elementary School Journal,* 1989, *89,* 301–342.

Pressley, M., and McCormick, C. *Advanced Educational Psychology for Educators, Researchers, and Policymakers.* New York: HarperCollins, 1995.

Resnick, L., Levine, J., and Teasley, S. (eds.). *Perspectives on Socially Shared Cognition.* Washington, D.C.: American Psychological Association, 1991.

Rhoads, R. A., and Howard, J.P.F. *Academic Service Learning: A Pedagogy of Action and Reflection.* New Directions for Teaching and Learning, no. 73. San Francisco: Jossey-Bass, 1998.

Schmeck, R. "Individual Differences and Learning Strategies." In C. E. Weinstein, E. Goetz, and P. Alexander (eds.), *Learning and Study Strategies: Issues in Assessment, Instruction, and Evaluation*. Orlando, Fla.: Academic Press, 1988a.

Schmeck, R. *Learning Strategies and Learning Styles*. New York: Plenum Press, 1988b.

Schunk, D. H., and Zimmerman, B. J. (eds.). *Self-Regulation of Learning and Performance: Issues and Educational Applications*. Mahwah, N.J.: Erlbaum, 1994.

Seligman, M. *Helplessness: On Depression, Development, and Death*. New York: Freeman, 1975.

Skinner, B. F. *Science and Human Behavior*. New York: Free Press, 1953.

Svinicki, M. D., and Dixon, N. M. "The Kolb Model Modified for Classroom Activities." *College Teaching*, 1987, *35*, 141–146.

Theall, M. *Motivation from Within: Encouraging Faculty and Students to Excel*. New Directions for Teaching and Learning, no. 78. San Francisco: Jossey-Bass, 1999.

Weiner, B. *Human Motivation*. Austin, Tex.: Holt, Rinehart and Winston, 1980.

Weiner, B. *An Attributional Theory of Motivation and Emotion*. New York: Springer-Verlag, 1986.

Weinstein, C. E. "Learning How to Learn: An Essential Skill for the 21st Century." *Educational Record*, 1996, *66*, 49–52.

Weinstein, C. E., Goetz, E., and Alexander, P. (eds.). *Learning and Study Strategies: Issues in Assessment, Instruction, and Evaluation*. Orlando, Fla.: Academic Press, 1988.

Weinstein, C. E., and Meyer, R. "The Teaching of Learning Strategies." In M. Wittrock (ed.), *The Handbook of Research on Teaching*. New York: Macmillan, 1986.

Wigfield, A., Eccles, J., and Pintrich, P. R. "Development Between the Ages of 11 and 25." In D. C. Berliner and R. C. Calfee (eds.), *Handbook of Educational Psychology*. New York: Macmillan, 1996.

Wilkerson, L., and Gijselaers, W. H. *Bringing Problem-Based Learning to Higher Education: Theory and Practice*. New Directions for Teaching and Learning, no. 68. San Francisco: Jossey-Bass, 1996.

Witkin, H., and Goodenough, D. *Cognitive Styles: Essence and Origins*. New York: International Universities Press, 1981.

MARILLA D. SVINICKI is editor-in-chief of the New Directions for Teaching and Learning *series and is director of the Center for Teaching Effectiveness and senior lecturer in the Department of Educational Psychology at the University of Texas at Austin.*

2

Half of the new directions being chronicled in this series apply to research on teaching. This chapter provides a thorough review of progress in research on teaching since 1980.

New Directions for Theory and Research on Teaching: A Review of the Past Twenty Years

Michael Theall

Given that over the past twenty years there has been increasing realization of the intimate connection between teaching and learning, it seems almost artificial to separate this chapter from Chapter One's review of the research on learning. Nevertheless, as Marilla Svinicki did with learning, I will attempt to discuss the research on teaching and to trace some of the important issues and findings of the past two decades. To simplify the task, I will consider six general areas related to higher education teaching:

- Teaching dimensions and behaviors
- Teaching considerations (including instructional design, methods, and teaching styles)
- Teaching and motivation
- Teaching and teacher assessment and evaluation
- Teaching technologies
- Teaching perspectives and philosophies

These areas are not discrete. The dimensions of teaching, for example, are general statements that can be explained or exemplified by considering the specific behaviors of teachers. These behaviors also relate to the teaching techniques determined by content needs, available resources, teacher skills and preferences, student characteristics, and other factors. Teacher preferences are in part determined by the experiences, philosophies, and underlying beliefs of individual teachers about teaching, learning, and their disciplines. Finally, the assessment and evaluation of teachers, teaching, and learning are intimately connected to the value systems, knowledge bases, experience, skills, and instructional objectives of each teacher.

It is no wonder, then, that the first descriptive term in Marsh's often-quoted overview of student evaluations of instruction is that evaluations and, by implication, teaching are "multidimensional" (1987). It is also clear that Doyle (1983) was correct when he made the cogent comment that "it seems most unlikely that any one set of characteristics will apply with equal force to the teaching of all kinds of material to all kinds of students under all kinds of circumstances" (p. 27). Consider the taxonomies of cognitive and affective instructional objectives developed by Bloom and others (1956) and Krathwohl, Bloom, and Masia (1956). Although objectives in the cognitive and affective domains can be carefully planned and exceptionally useful, one must acknowledge that teachers cannot rigidly adhere to any predetermined list. As Jean Civikly-Powell notes in Chapter Four, teaching and learning involve human communication and interactions, and consequently, they are subject to all the forces that affect human behavior. Particularly in the public arena of the classroom, situations arise that require immediate actions or reactions, often in the affective domain. Teachers cannot plan for all such contingencies. How do teachers maintain control, a positive atmosphere, and students' interest level—and do all that in an organized, coherent, and effective manner? Classrooms are places of constant change, and teaching involves adapting to this fluctuating reality.

A recent study (Chiu, Wardrop, and Ryan, 1999) reported findings consistent with previous research that student ratings of instruction can account for approximately 40 percent of the variance in a determination of teaching effectiveness. What of the other 60 percent? What, indeed, is *teaching effectiveness?* Factors beyond the teacher's control (student ability, prior preparation, value systems, and personal considerations, for example) can greatly affect instructional outcomes. Should we hold teachers responsible for 100 percent of the results of a course of instruction, or would it be more realistic and fair, perhaps, to hold them responsible only for the 40 percent that can be attributed to their influence? When we talk of effective teaching, what we cannot find in the literature is a simple or generalizable definition or any absolute measurement criterion.

In sum, we can say that teaching is complex, multidimensional, and dynamic. It is profoundly affected by the individuals involved in the process as well as by circumstances beyond the classroom. No wonder, then, that *effective teaching* has been difficult to define, describe, and measure in concrete and absolute terms.

Dimensions of Teaching and Teaching Behaviors

Perhaps the most frequently discussed strategy for understanding teaching has been to try to identify the critical dimensions of teaching.

Dimensions of Teaching. What do we know about college teaching? One way to explore this question is to consider the relationship of various aspects of teaching to common performance criteria and to ask the people involved in it to identify the important issues. This research on the "dimensions" of teaching has come from studies in which students or faculty were asked to identify or rank important aspects of teaching (for example, Crittenden and Norr, 1973) and from the analyses of student ratings data and other data (for example, as reported by Centra, 1979). Several factors have appeared consistently and repeatedly. Marsh and Hocevar (1984) reported the following to be "factorially invariant": amount learned or value of the course, enthusiasm, organization, group interaction, individual rapport, breadth of coverage, examinations, assignments, and level of work or difficulty. Assembling work in these areas, Feldman (1989) conducted meta-analyses of studies of correlations between dimensions of teaching and achievement and correlations of the dimensions of teaching with student ratings. He also compiled results from studies asking faculty and students to rank the importance of the dimensions of instruction. Although the results are too complex to review here, it would be fair to summarize them by saying that there are some aspects of teaching that are consistently related to achievement and are identified by teachers and students alike as important, and there are some aspects where just the opposite is true. Likewise, there are aspects on which students and faculty agree and others on which they disagree.

Though these results may seem contradictory and somewhat confusing, they point to another important notion: that not every teacher must be expert in every dimension in order to be effective, successful, or highly rated. Hativa (1999a) recently made this point in an exploration of the behaviors of teachers. She noted that her subjects used different strategies to achieve their goals. Franklin and Theall (1992) reported disciplinary differences in choices of instructional objectives and in teaching and assessment methods. Although the patterns of choices matched the patterns of rankings of disciplines based on average ratings of teachers and courses (Cashin, 1990), the findings supported the notion that good teaching takes many forms and cannot be limited to only a few methods or dimensions. Michael Scriven (personal communication, Nov. 9, 1998) has suggested that equitable faculty evaluation cannot be based on the assumption that teachers who address certain of the dimensions are effective and those who do not address these dimensions are ineffective. In other words, we have established correlation but not causation, and we have not yet developed absolute criteria for effectiveness.

It is probably safe to say that in traditional teaching and learning situations, the essential dimensions of college teaching have been identified and their relationship to teaching effectiveness has been established. Attention to these dimensions will likely result in more effective instruction, and ignoring them risks reducing effectiveness. There is little research providing insight into the newest instructional delivery strategies: the various forms of distance education and, particularly, asynchronous instruction.

Teaching Behaviors. At one level of specificity below the dimensions, we find considerable research on the more discrete behaviors of teachers. Primarily the work of Murray and his associates (discussed in Murray, 1983, and summarized in Murray, 1991), these studies have identified *low-inference* behaviors: specific, observable teacher behaviors that can be recorded without the need for a researcher or an observer to makes inferences from other behaviors. *Clarity,* for example, is an important dimension of teaching. One low-inference behavior that promotes the clarity of presentations is to use concrete examples to help describe concepts. The research has attempted to identify other such behaviors in order to provide more specific guidelines and strategies for teachers.

Furthering this line of thinking, Hativa (1999b) differentiated low-inference behaviors from high- and intermediate-inference behaviors, proposing a four-level model. The main dimension of clarity can be broken down, for example, into intermediate behaviors including "simplifying the material presented," which can then include more specific behaviors such as "teaching in two or more cycles." This behavior can be further broken down to include "presenting a concrete case prior to discussing an abstract principle," "presenting a comparable case, analogy, or metaphor for the concept," or "presenting a visual, intuitive, or other interpretation of the concept."

The specific behaviors described by Hativa (1999b) are in one sense examples of what Shulman (1986, 1989) has called "pedagogical content knowledge." This knowledge combines an understanding of effective pedagogies with deep subject knowledge and includes a clear and solid grasp of the basic principles of the discipline; the ability to explain complex concepts simply; having a well-developed and available repertoire of alternative explanations, methods, or techniques; and the ability to diagnose students' problems and offer solutions.

As investigations of specific behaviors of effective teachers get more detailed and precise and as they expand to include a variety of disciplines and teaching and learning situations, our understanding of the dynamics of instruction will increase and more opportunities will be created to test the applicability of low-inference behaviors under a variety of instructional conditions. Those that prove generally useful can be disseminated by means of publications, institutional centers for teaching and learning, professional associations, and electronic and personal networks to a wide faculty audience for incorporation into day-to-day practice.

Teaching Considerations

Beyond understanding what qualities and behaviors are involved in teaching, much attention has been paid to the variables an instructor must consider when designing instruction.

Instructional Design. Though instruction is facilitated by knowing specific techniques that relate to specific dimensions of teaching, it is not sufficient to think only of these discrete skills. Effective teaching involves assembling the set of materials, circumstances, tools, stimuli, processes, and alternatives that have the greatest potential to contribute to the achievement of the instructors' (and sometimes the students') objectives. It is therefore reasonable to consider the design of instruction from a systems perspective (Bethany, 1987; Diamond, 1989; Reigeluth, 1983).

Few faculty, however, have any formal training or experience in the design, development, or evaluation of instruction. As Stark and others have reported (1988), faculty are most often influenced by their academic disciplines, their personal beliefs, and their own backgrounds. Franklin and Theall (1992) also found very consistent patterns of instructional choices within disciplines.

Further evidence comes from Smart and Feldman (1998), who, using the theory of Holland (1985), found evidence that matches or mismatches of individuals to "academic subenvironments can be an especially potent source of influence on students" (p. 416). In other words, students become acculturated to or affiliated with their departments and their disciplines. They likely adopt faculty habits of thought and attitudes, and if they move on to faculty positions, they seem largely to teach in the ways they were taught. Though such continuity can give rise to questions about openness to new ideas or methods, my comment is not pejorative with respect to teaching in these disciplines. Instead, as Shulman's pedagogical content knowledge paradigm (1987) implies, deep knowledge of the subject matter is an essential element in understanding how best to teach that subject matter. The phenomenon does help explain, however, traditional faculty resistance to "teaching improvement" efforts coming from outside the discipline.

The field of systematic instructional design nonetheless offers a broadly applicable and generalizable model for instruction because it considers the many systems that can influence instructional decisions and outcomes and because when properly applied, it requires the instructor to view teaching and learning ecologically, rather than concentrating solely on disciplinary content. Given that few faculty (especially new faculty) have developed true pedagogical content knowledge, the combination of the instructor's content knowledge with the structure of the design process and assistance from pedagogical experts (instructional consultants, as in Brinko and Menges, 1997) is a most effective way to engender genuine pedagogical content knowledge and to develop the expertise of faculty more quickly.

Teaching Methods. A second area, which is more closely examined in the literature, is that of methods of teaching. For most of its history, teaching in higher education has been fairly traditional. Over the past twenty years, however, more and more alternatives have been introduced and deserve consideration.

Traditional Methods. Numerous resources deal with traditional approaches such as lecturing, discussion, and case, laboratory, and clinical methods. Major works providing guidelines include Davis, 1993; Lowman,

1984; and McKeachie, 1999b, but a full review of all these methods is beyond the scope of this chapter.

Active and Cooperative Learning Methods. McKeachie (1999a, 1999b) has suggested that the most widespread and successful techniques for teaching can be gathered under the banner of *active learning.* Whether the method involves others (as in *collaborative learning, cooperative learning, teaming,* or *group work*) or focuses on the investigative process (as in *discovery learning* or *problem-based learning*), the essential concept is the active and often cooperative involvement of students in the processes of finding, analyzing, evaluating, synthesizing, and applying information. In particular, cooperative methods (for example, Johnson and Johnson, 1988; Johnson, Johnson, and Smith, 1991) seem to have additional motivational advantages (McKinnon, 1999; Panitz, 1999). According to Davis (1993), "Researchers report that, regardless of the subject matter, students working in small groups tends to learn more of what is taught and retain it longer than when the same content is presented in other instructional formats" (p. 147). Discussion of these types of methods can be found in several of the *New Directions* issues, including issues 59 on collaborative learning, 61 on gateway courses, 63 on self-regulated learning, 67 on active learning, and 68 on problem-based learning. The *New Directions* series in general has attempted to bring brief introductions to the newest methods as they begin to take hold, so this series is a good resource for information about individual methods.

Technology-Based Methods. There is little definitive guidance for distance education and, particularly, teaching in asynchronous modes. Two *New Directions* issues (51 and 71) deal with this topic, and we will return to the topic later in this chapter.

Teaching and Learning Styles. Teaching style is a topic that of necessity overlaps with learning style, and approaches to style are numerous. Some observers have argued that the term *style* is incorrectly applied and that *preferences* is more appropriate in many cases. For example, there are some individuals who prefer to work in quiet or warm or brightly lit environments as opposed to noisy or cool or dimly lit locations. These preferences are not necessarily *styles* of teaching or learning, but they do indicate that individuals have considered their own experiences and made choices about the situations in which they feel most capable. If they have been successful in these environments, they tend to seek out such conditions again. Nevertheless, there are differences that go beyond preference and into information processing capabilities, organizational ability, cultural differences, and even physiological and neurological structures. For inclusiveness, I will use the term *individual differences* to refer to the broad range of topics covered, but I will concentrate on how these differences affect teaching. (Discussion of their impact on learning appears in Chapter One.)

Teaching and Learning Styles. One source of information that is current and specifically targets instructional practice is Anthony Grasha's *Teaching with Style* (1996). This work is rich with illustrations, examples, and exercises that teachers can use effectively. Grasha offers several models of individual differences. The basic model has three bipolar constructs— *competitive–collaborative, dependent–independent,* and *participant–avoidant*— that relate to individual differences in the behaviors and approaches among learners. Here is a short description of the characteristics of these types of individuals:

Competitive = learns in order to perform or excel; seeks recognition; likes to lead

Collaborative = likes to share; seeks involvement; likes projects and group work

Dependent = shows little curiosity; does only what is expected or required; seeks help from peers or teachers; dislikes ambiguity; likes structure imposed

Independent = is usually confident; thinks for oneself; likes to work alone; likes self-paced work

Participant = is a good citizen; joins in; likes to discuss; likes optional work; is eager

Avoidant = is not enthusiastic; does not join in; dislikes testing; does not like being called on

More important for its relationship to teaching, Grasha also uses the inventory devised by Myers (1990) to classify several dimensions of teacher activities necessary to execute various instructional methods and presents an array of *roles* for teachers. He also reviews many other dimensions of individual differences among teachers and students and provides several inventories and exercises that help define differences.

Experiential Models. Perhaps the most widely known experiential model to link style differences with teaching methods is that of Kolb (1984). Its essential learner dimensions are *concrete–abstract* and *reflective–active.* In a 2 × 2 matrix, the combinations of the components lead to identification of learners as accommodators (concrete, active), divergers (concrete, reflective), assimilators (abstract, reflective), and convergers (abstract, active). Its application to teaching and learning is well exemplified by Svinicki and Dixon (1987), who propose a cycle of learning that moves from experience to observation to conceptualization to experimentation. They provide sample instructional sequences that show how, in various disciplines, instruction can provide learners with opportunities to capitalize on their strengths.

Classroom Dynamics and Pedagogical Styles. Hardy (1976) identified four teacher styles: *discipline-centered, instructor-centered, student-centered cognitive,* and *student-centered affective.* The titles are largely self-descriptive and relate to other descriptions of faculty roles (including Grasha's). Grasha (1996) proposes that the essential faculty roles are *expert, formal authority, personal model, delegator,* and *facilitator.* Again, these titles are largely self-explanatory, as are various descriptions of classroom dynamics, which commonly use terms such as *autocratic, democratic,* and *anarchic.* The instructor's style clearly determines the nature of the classroom dynamic and, depending on its interaction with other factors already discussed, can either match learner styles and disciplinary affect with positive results or conflict with learner and disciplinary styles with negative results.

Motivation and Teaching

Like design, methods, and style, motivation is an extremely broad area of teaching. Motivational techniques vary as much and as often as the situations in which they are used. However, there seem to be some major themes that are part of the motivational models developed by several writers. Table 2.1, reprinted from *New Directions* volume 78, arrays the work of contributors to that volume as well as other conceptions of motivation and closely related work. The thrust of that volume and the terms in the table are toward intrinsic motivation: the establishing of conditions that enhance teachers' or students' innate desire, interest, and willingness to expend effort and receive satisfaction from instructional or other tasks and subsequent outcomes. In other words, seeking strategies that connect with existing interests and providing opportunities for students to take an active part in the instruction can lead to increased involvement, effort, and eventual success. The resulting motivation is intrinsic because it targets the deeper "learning orientation" of students rather than the superficial "grade orientation."

This view differs from older conceptions that regarded motivation as something "done" to someone, a response to an imposed set of extrinsic rewards, more in the behaviorist mode, as discussed in Chapter One. In Table 2.2, the left-hand column presents the six terms examined in Table 2.1, derived from the work of the same authors shown in the top row. The cells of the table that are marked with a capital X indicate that the author used the term shown or an analogous term with almost the same meaning. The cells marked with a lowercase x indicate situations where the author's work could, with little elaboration, be said to include the term on the left. As a scan of the table shows, certain general terms apply directly in almost every model, and the remaining terms fill literally the rest of the cells. The sole exception (Pintrich and others, 1988) exists because the model used was the Motivated Strategies for Learning Questionnaire (MSLQ), which does not include items on inclusion and leadership. However, Pintrich's later work on "self-regulation" (1995) has strong implications for the use of intrinsic motivational strategies. These connect well with studies by Perry and his colleagues on perceived control and attributional issues (Perry, 1991) and particularly with his work on "attributional retraining" (Menec and others, 1994), which has proved especially effective for students with a history of academic difficulties.

Table 2.1. Motivation Terms: Author by Factor Matrix

Author / Factor	Wlodkowski	Paulsen[a]	Donald	Keller	MacKinnon	Panitz	Feldman[b]	Nuhfer	Farmer	Theall[c]	Pintrich	Forsyth[d]	Chickering[e]
Inclusion	X												
Community						X	X			X		X	X
Climate			X		X		X						X
Ownership		X			X		X	X					X
Attitude	X												
Affect		X	X			X							
Interest										X	X		X
Awareness			X					X	X				
Attention				X				X	X				
Enthusiasm													
Meaning	X												
Relevance		X	X	X	X					X	X	X	X
Value										X			X
Competence	X												
Empowerment		X			X	X						X	
Confidence		X		X								X	
Expectancy			X							X	X		
Leadership													
High expectations			X			X	X		X	X		X	X
Structure								X		X			X
Feedback							X	X		X			
Support							X						
Satisfaction													
Rewards				X		X			X			X	

[a] Paulsen and Feldman, 1999.
[b] Feldman and Paulsen, 1999.
[c] Theall, Birdsall, and Franklin, 1997.
[d] Forsyth and McMillan, 1991.
[e] Chickering and Gamson, 1987.
Source: Theall and Franklin, 1999, p. 101. Used by permission of Jossey-Bass Inc., Publishers.

Table 2.2. Key Motivation Terms: Author by Factor Matrix

Author Factor	Wlodkowski	Paulsen[a]	Donald	Keller	MacKinnon	Panitz	Feldman[b]	Nuhfer	Farmer	Theall[c]	Pintrich	Forsyth[d]	Chickering[e]
Inclusion	X	X	X	x	X	X	X	X	X	X		X	X
Attitude	X	X	X	X	x	X	x	X	x	X	X	x	X
Meaning	X	X	X	X	X	x	x	x	x	X	X	X	X
Competence	X	X	X	X	X	X	X	X	x	X	X	X	x
Leadership	x	x	X	x	x	x	X	X	X	X		X	X
Satisfaction	x	x	x	X	x	X	x	x	X		x	X	x

[a]Paulsen and Feldman, 1999.
[b]Feldman and Paulsen, 1999.
[c]Theall, Birdsall, and Franklin, 1997.
[d]Forsyth and McMillan, 1991.
[e]Chickering and Gamson, 1987.

Source: Theall and Franklin, 1999, p. 106. Used by permission of Jossey-Bass Inc., Publishers.

The consistency of the constructs used in these thirteen different models is striking and powerful, but the terms are, of course, general. For teachers who seek a detailed description of the application of a model to the specific task of designing instruction, Keller's ARCS model (1987) offers a workable design. Beginning with *attention* strategies, the model stresses *relevance,* the development of students' *confidence* in positive outcomes, and their eventual *satisfaction* as a result of positive performance. Greater effort consistently leads to improved performance, and improved performance leads to satisfaction. The cycle continues as satisfaction enhances the student's valuing the content and having raised expectancy for further success. A positive cycle of intrinsic motivation results, and performance is improved. Teachers could conceivably intervene at any step along the way to increase student motivation.

Assessment and Evaluation of Teachers and Teaching

Perhaps the most influential work in assessment, especially as regards classroom techniques, is that of Angelo and Cross (1993). Based on an earlier report from the National Center for Research to Improve Postsecondary Teaching and Learning (NCRIPTAL) at the University of Michigan (Cross and Angelo, 1988), the text attempts to "respond directly to concerns about better learning and more effective teaching" (Angelo and Cross, 1993, p. xiii) rather than the broader issues of the "assessment movement," which focuses more on the gathering and use of evidence about the outcomes of education and the degree to which institutions are successfully preparing students for careers and for life.

Angelo and Cross (1993) offer hundreds of strategies, tips, hints, procedures, and methods to teachers, focusing on assessing skills such as recall, understanding, critical thinking, creative thinking, problem solving, application, attitudes, and self-awareness. The underlying relationship of assessment to instructional design is obvious, as these techniques require the teacher to know and to have previously articulated specific plans and objectives for instruction. As the old saying goes, "If you don't know where you're going, you won't know if or when you get there." Though many authorities decry the development of instructional objectives as a mechanistic and formulaic process, the essential focus is not on the objective itself but rather on the specification of what the learner must be able to do at the completion of the instruction. Knowing the intended outcome greatly facilitates the development of instructional strategies and the determination of the measures that will provide evidence of achievement.

Many of the techniques reviewed by Angelo and Cross (1993) come from the literature of faculty development, evaluation, and teaching improvement. For example, the process known as *small group instructional diagnosis* (SGID) uses a focus group technique to extract critical information about the success of instruction. Originally proposed by Clark and Bekey (1979), SGID has been used extensively in formative assessment and evaluation, and in combination with quantitative instruments (such as validated student ratings questionnaires), it is a powerful tool for understanding classroom process, dynamics, and effectiveness. Another widely used technique is the *one-minute paper,* first reported by Wilson (1986) in his investigations of faculty techniques for improving teaching. This technique and its several variations simply ask students to take a very small amount of time to answer one or two questions at the end of a class period. Usually, students are asked to tell "the most important thing you learned today" or to tell about "something you did not understand in today's class." Feedback about students' understanding (or lack of it) helps teachers plan for the short term ("What do I do in our next class?") and also for the long term ("Should I build in extra time next semester for a hands-on project that will make the concept more clear?" or "I should do this again. It worked very well").

The conceptual and procedural distances between assessment and evaluation are not great. Both are processes for gathering and using data appropriately and effectively, and indeed, the two can be and should be complementary. For example, the terms *formative* and *summative* originally proposed by Scriven (1967) to describe the roles of evaluation, are used with the identical meaning in both fields: *formative* for improvement or revision and *summative* for making decisions about merit or worth. In the same work, Scriven also proposed two other terms that are less used but equally important: *instrumental* and *consequential*. These refer to the processes of instruction and its outcomes. Complete assessment or evaluation should consider these aspects of instruction as well as the purposes of the assessment or evaluation. Role determination not only clarifies the intended use of the data but also guides the process and procedures chosen, as well as the choice of how and to whom the results are reported.

Thus to propose any major dichotomy between assessment and evaluation seems almost foolish, given that the assessment of instructional outcomes is crucial to the evaluation of individual and program success. Student achievement is, after all, the intent of instruction and should be part of the data set used in making determinations about the success of instruction and instructional programs as well as the process of awarding grades and degrees.

A problem arises, however, when the focus of evaluation is the rating of teaching performance or, even more problematic, overall faculty performance. The problem is primarily in the area of the quality of evaluation practice, and the greatest error made today is the use of a single data source (for example, student ratings of instruction) as the basis for decision making. While the continuous debate about faculty evaluation rages on and is often phrased in terms that attack the validity and reliability of student ratings, the ultimate problem is poor practice and the lack of knowledge of evaluation among the individuals who use and interpret the data (Franklin and Theall, 1989). Many variables have been cited as potentially biasing factors in student ratings, but the consistent findings of the research are best summarized by Marsh (1987), who said that student ratings are "(1) multidimensional; (2) reliable and stable; (3) primarily a function of the instructor who teaches a course rather than the course that is taught; (4) relatively valid against a variety of indicators of effective teaching; (5) relatively unaffected by a variety of indicators hypothesized as potential biases; and (6) seen to be useful by faculty, by students, and by administrators" (p. 255).

Given the interest in outcomes in both evaluation and assessment, one of the most important issues is instructional effectiveness in terms of student learning, and one of the powerful arguments for the validity of student ratings comes from Cohen's study (1981), which considered multisection courses with identical midterm exams administered and graded by someone other than the section instructor. The meta-analysis of several studies of multisection courses revealed a correlation of .43 between ratings and achievement on the exams; that is to say, there was a strong and significant relationship between ratings and learning. Though there is considerable current debate about some issues, no substantial and consistent evidence yet exists to deny the ratings-learning relationship. In other words, good teaching leads to good learning, and good learning results in good grades and satisfied students. This does not mean, however, that the topic is exempt of debate.

One contentious topic is the effect of "grade inflation" on ratings. Some research (Greenwald and Gillmore, 1997a, 1997b) claims that statistical controls and special data reporting formats can reduce or remove this supposed "contaminant" of ratings, but there is strong opposition to these conclusions (Franklin and Theall, 1991; Gillmore and others, 1998). Another sensitive topic is gender. Despite numerous studies showing that on the whole, neither student nor faculty gender directly affects ratings in a significant way (Centra and Gaubatz, 1998; Feldman, 1992a, 1992b; Franklin and Theall, 1994), a debate continues over gender bias. Interestingly, the gender bias that was found was in the assignment of female instructors to difficult teaching situations in one department at one institution (Franklin and Theall, 1994). Women were a minority in the department and were disproportionately assigned to large undergraduate required classes. These kinds of classes show consistent patterns of slightly lower ratings for all faculty; thus anyone teaching such classes could expect depressed ratings. If course assignments were deliberate and ratings results were uncritically examined, one could mistakenly attribute lower ratings either to poor performance by females or to student bias against females: both conclusions would be erroneous. In fact, when the study was replicated in the same departments at another institution of similar size where the course assignment patterns were equitable, women had slightly higher average ratings than men (Franklin and Theall, 1994).

More than twenty-five hundred studies, papers, articles, and books have been written on the subject of faculty evaluation. Although the vast majority of these (particularly those undergoing rigorous review) have shown ratings to be reliable, valid, and useful, there has been disproportionate discussion of flawed or small sample studies, possibly because faculty are rightfully concerned about the impact of ratings on their careers. Given the poor state of practice, it is no wonder that faculty are suspicious of the evaluation process and argue against its primary data source: student evaluations.

A more reasonable approach is that offered by Arreola (1994) and in line with Miller's earlier ten principles for evaluation (1987). Both emphasize the cooperative development of complete "systems" for faculty evaluation. Crucial to this process is participation in the identification of performance areas and criteria and the determination of who will provide what data to whom. A priori agreement about these issues among all concerned parties (faculty, administrators, students, or others) is necessary before questionnaires are adopted or developed.

Whatever processes, procedures, and policies for assessment and evaluation are selected, they must reflect institutional and individual needs and the concerns of all constituencies. Imposed questionnaires, inappropriate or poorly constructed reports, unvalidated questionnaires, insecure data handling processes, and marginal data management all contribute to poor practice. Even more, institutional affect will determine the reaction of faculty and students to the evaluation process. If good teaching goes unrewarded and if evaluation results are used only when they are negative, faculty will resist evaluation, and with good reason. If evaluations are disregarded and if students perceive that their input is unheeded, they will not be motivated to provide complete and thoughtful responses. In either case, evaluation is counterproductive. Aleamoni (1987) and Theall and Franklin (1990, 1991) have outlined both general and specific guidelines for evaluating and improving teaching using student ratings and other evaluative data. The sought-for system is one that provides accurate, reliable, and useful data to persons who can correctly interpret and fairly use that data. Anything less destroys the true potential of evaluation to serve its many constituencies.

Teaching and Technology

The impact of technology on teaching and learning has been questioned at least since books became readily available to students. The massive investigation of the relationship of technology and teaching has taken place in the past half-century with military studies of film and other media followed by a spate of television studies in the 1950s and 1960s. The result: essentially nothing. The majority of studies found no significant or widespread effects of technology on learning (Chu and Schramm, 1967). An early critic (Mielke, 1968) suggested that the underlying questions of such comparative research were inappropriate because the compared situations were essentially identical to begin with. A lecture in one room was still a lecture in the next room, even though the instructor was present in one case and televised in the other.

The next wave of studies began with distance education via video technologies such as cable television and ITFS (instructional television fixed service: microwave-spectrum space reserved for educational use). Some positive results were reported, for example, by Gibbons, Kinchloe, and Down (1977), who described an ITFS-delivered program of graduate engineering courses in which students at distant sites outperformed those on campus. However, the design of the instruction included the use of an on-site tutor in combination with live broadcasts and the ability to review taped lectures. The positive results could not be attributed simply to the use of television; rather, they were due to the effective design of the courses and the combination of media and a set of other resources.

TV research was soon overtaken by investigations into the use and effectiveness of computers. Again, a major error was made: the assumption that it would be possible to find some difference between "traditional" instruction and instruction that used some form of mediation. The mistakes made with television were repeated with computers, often with the same results. These have been documented by Russell (1999), who reports 355 studies showing no significant differences.

The most credible research took its approach from Cronbach and Snow's work on "aptitude treatment interactions" (1969) and considered the specific effects of the unique attributes of the medium in question with relation to particular cognitive and task requirements. Salomon's work, culminating in his *Interaction of Media, Cognition, and Learning* (1969), is probably the most established and well conceptualized in this area, as he was able to demonstrate the use of technology to "compensate for" or "remediate" or "supplant" certain cognitive processes for students. The gains were a result of an appropriate match between instructional needs and available technological tools that had the capability to present information in ways impossible in a traditional instructional mode.

In a meta-analysis of technology and college teaching studies (including personalized systems of instruction and autotutorial instruction), Kulik, Kulik, and Cohen (1980) found that "instructional technology had a positive impact on course outcome in most of the studies" and that "the overall results suggest that experimentation with instructional technology is worthwhile. . . . It would be foolish, however, to pretend that the effects of instructional technology are large ones" (pp. 201, 204). Richard Clark (1983) "reconsidered research on learning from media" and concluded, "One might reasonably wonder why media are still advocated for their ability to increase learning when research clearly indicates that such benefits are not forthcoming" (p. 456).

In the past twenty years, however, there have been some changes. Clark himself, in the introduction to Russell's book (1999), says, "The most promising of the new directions can be found in a study of potential eco-nomic benefits from various media. If media researchers and practitioners would only switch their concerns to the economics of instruction, we would discover all manner of important cost contributions from media" (p. xi). Whether cost contributions are sufficient to promote widespread acceptance of technology remains to be seen. Though administrators and trustees see cost benefits as desirable, faculty often see them as a cost-cutting rationale leading to the loss of teaching positions.

What does current research on teaching with emerging technologies tell us? At this point, nothing very definitive. When we find situations, as Clark suggested, that capitalize on the unique attributes of technology for a matching instructional need, what we have found amounts to good instruc-tional design, that is, choosing the right tool for the right job. Indeed, although there is much research on the use of technology, there is much less definitive research on whether new technologies, especially asynchronous technologies used in distance education, can be said to enhance learning simply by virtue of their use. To paraphrase Clark, it isn't the delivery truck that nourishes you, it's the food that it brings. In the same vein, well-designed instruction that appropriately uses technology can provide end-less opportunities for teachers and students, opportunities never before possible. But the haphazard application of technology for its own sake can just as well result in "no significant difference" or, worse, the disillusion-ment of teachers and students and yet another cycle of expensive technol-ogy relegated to storage closets.

Perspectives on Teaching

Lest it be said that the past twenty years have concentrated solely on mech-anistic, technical, or quantitative issues related to teaching, some reference needs to be made to the ongoing dialogue about teachers and teaching—about the people, the profession, the priorities, and the practice. Ernest Boyer's Carnegie Foundation report (1990) has been one of the most influ-ential discussions of the professoriate and of the nature of scholarship. The report outlines the changing directions of higher education and the pres-sures on professors at various types of institutions. Boyer defines four kinds of scholarship: the scholarship of discovery, which "contributes not only to the stock of human knowledge but also to the intellectual climate of the uni-versity"; the scholarship of integration, which makes "connections across the disciplines, placing the specialties in a larger context, illuminating data in a revealing way, often educating nonspecialists too"; the scholarship of application, which "moves toward engagement" where "new intellectual understandings can arise out of the very act of application"; and the schol-arship of teaching, where "the work of the professor becomes consequen-tial only as it is understood by others" (pp. 17–23).

Carnegie studies revealed that the scholarship of discovery was pre-eminent, especially with respect to its importance at research and doctoral institutions. Decisions about faculty performance were based largely on scholarly output, though effective teaching performance (however documented) was expected nonetheless. The problem for many faculty was (and is) that good teaching is not adequately rewarded while poor teaching is often used as a reason for denial of promotion or tenure or even for dismissal. Robert Boice's work (for example, 1991, 1992) addresses the problems new faculty face in balancing the requirement to produce scholarship of many kinds and offers guidelines that can help new faculty become "quick starters." More distressing is Machell's report of "'professorial melancholia,' a progressive emotional process characterized by the negating of a university professor's professional motivation, positive attitudinal focus, and adequate personal self-esteem" (1989, p. 41). This destructive cycle can best be avoided through institutional attention to the needs of teachers and students (Farmer, 1999) and the development of a "supportive teaching culture" as described by Feldman and Paulsen (1999).

What do these discussions of scholarship and professional pressure have to do with teaching? Part of the answer is related to the cyclical emphasis on supporting effective teaching. In the 1960s and 1970s, many centers for teaching were created. By the late 1970s and early 1980s, institutional programs and resources for the support of teaching had diminished, and nearly every one of these centers (even some with national reputations) had closed. Ironically, literature on teaching abounded, and teachers could select from a wide array of resources, as documented by Menges and Mathis (1988).

In the past decade, we have seen renewed interest in support for teachers and teaching. Although external funding like that available for teaching centers in the 1960s has not been the mode, it is heartening to see that many institutions have taken on the responsibility of supporting both teaching and learning. Boyer's distinctions were important in bringing about this emphasis. There has been much discussion, especially of the scholarship of teaching, and work is in fact under way on a *New Directions* volume devoted to this topic.

Other writers have profoundly influenced our conception of teaching in the past twenty years. Pascarella and Terenzini (1991), in their landmark work on the effects of college on students, established the importance of the teaching and learning environment and the impact of student-teacher interactions beyond the classroom. From this and work mentioned elsewhere in this chapter came Chickering and Gamson's *Applying the Seven Principles for Good Practice in Undergraduate Education* (1991), revisited by the authors in Chapter Six of this volume and one of the most cited and influential guidelines for higher education of the decade. Though not proposing to offer extensive and detailed suggestions for teachers, the principles suggest the importance of interaction, cooperation, engagement, task orientation, communication, feedback, and mutual respect to successful teaching and learning. The principles and the work that underlies them are powerful indicators that teaching involves more than presenting information to a passive audience.

Another notable voice in the dialogue has been Donald Schön (1983, 1991), who argued for "an epistemology of practice based on reflection-in-action" and proposed a reflective practicum where "students mainly learn by doing, with the help of coaching" (1991, p. xii). The reflective practitioner approach mirrors the active learning emphasis noted earlier and reinforces the importance of engagement, time on task, and the ongoing partnership of students and teachers ("apprentices and masters" or "interns and mentors" might be appropriate descriptive terms). The mutually reinforcing concepts from all these writers serve to stress the intellectual and role model responsibilities of teachers and the extension of teaching beyond the simple need to "profess." A particularly interesting and relevant set of essays can be found in *The Social Worlds of Higher Education: Handbook for Teaching in a New Century* (Pescosolido and Aminzade, 1999), a work based on three premises: that "the institution of higher education is undergoing radical shifts," that "these shifts reflect not only changes in theories of teaching and learning, but large changes in society," and that "the improvement of teaching will require a broad, concerted, and truly multidisciplinary effort" (p. 13). The combination of a very broad range of perspectives and a "field guide" of useful hints provides both theoretical and practical information for teachers and makes this a timely and thought-provoking work.

An even further elaboration of non-subject-bound teaching emphasis comes from Parker Palmer (1983, 1997). Palmer exhorts teachers to involve themselves in teaching in deep and personal ways, offering the personal perspective quoted by Jean Civikly-Powell in Chapter Four of this volume: "As I teach, I project the condition of my soul onto my students, my subject, and our way of being together" (1997, p. 15). Palmer's words have inspired many to develop philosophies or perspectives on teaching that are humanistic and student-centered. An example is a list of "commandments" proposed by Louis Schmier (personal communication, Oct. 12, 1998) on the theme "teach to that one student," which includes admonitions to teach "with an unshakable faith, with unconditional love, with bold courage, with boundless energy, with uncompromising tenacity, and with your spirit anchored in unending hope."

Such personal statements focus as much on the teacher's human responsibilities toward students as they do on professional, disciplinary, or even institutional needs. They have become more common partly as a result of the interest in teaching *dossiers* (Shore and others, 1986) and *portfolios* (Seldin, 1991) and the recommended inclusion of statements of philosophy in these compilations. There are many sources of information and even electronically accessible guides for the preparation of such statements (see, for example, Haugen, 1998).

Although such presentations of personal philosophy and perspectives are important and help illuminate the approaches and values of teachers, they raise a different kind of difficult question: How do we incorporate and consider such statements into the necessary decision-making processes? In an invited address at the annual meeting of the American Educational Research Association, Larry Braskamp (1999) stressed the "integrity" of good teachers and teaching and discussed struggling with the concept with respect to promoting it as a vital part of institutional thinking about teaching and to the difficulties of measuring it as an indicator of excellence. His comments highlight both the importance of establishing and sharing perspectives on teaching and the complexities of arriving at shared definitions and perspectives in an arena so broad and diversified. Clearly, the traditional autonomy granted teachers and the need to preserve an appropriate degree of academic freedom must be balanced against the reality that making judgments about teacher performance includes the need to establish benchmarks. In the arena of personal philosophies, this becomes a very difficult conceptual, political, and practical task.

Ultimately, some observers may reach the conclusion that teaching is so personal, intimate, and individualistic that it defies description or measurement. This would be an unfortunate error, for it would misunderstand concepts like pedagogical content knowledge, it would fly in the face of Boyer's definitions of scholarship, and it would result in chaos when decisions about merit or worth had to be made. Teaching will always include the uniqueness of the individuals (teachers and students) who are involved, but it will also include process, techniques, strategies, and methods that can be successfully investigated and then replicated across situations, disciplines, classrooms, and contexts. The "scholarship of teaching" seeks to celebrate the accomplishments of individuals but also to identify concepts, principles, and ideas that have merit and to share them with a wide constituency.

Conclusion

In this chapter, I have attempted to review two decades of research relating to many important aspects of college teaching. In the process, it became clear that it is impossible to separate teaching from learning in any reasonable way. Not only this, but it is particularly difficult to treat teaching as a discrete topic divorced from the many other factors that influence the overall dynamics of classrooms, offices, lounges, cafeterias, buildings, and campuses. In other words, this chapter reinforced the notion that college teaching and learning take place in a complex and ever-changing environment, a community affected by and affecting the larger world. As Pascarella and Terenzini (1991) point out, it is the overall experience of college that affects students, and college is, as Pescosolido and Aminzade (1999) also point out, a "social world" that greatly influences both teaching and learning.

A good starting place to consider the array of research on college teaching is Feldman and Paulsen's *Teaching and Learning in the College Classroom* (1998). From it one can get a glimpse of the many multiple interacting forces and variables at work in higher education, and one can begin to see how interdependent these variables are. Perhaps the notion of research on "ecollegy" is appropriate, for these separate systems must be balanced and interact productively if higher education is to succeed.

What, then, does the research of the past two decades tell us? I believe it tells us that we all have much to learn and much to do if we are to achieve the lofty ideals found in admissions brochures and in our hearts. It also gives us hope that exciting new techniques, discoveries, technologies, and strategies can improve both teaching and learning. And it tells us that two decades of research is just the beginning of a long and necessary but exciting journey into what we are only beginning to know.

References

Aleamoni, L. M. (ed.). *Techniques for Evaluating and Improving Instruction.* New Directions for Teaching and Learning, no. 31. San Francisco: Jossey-Bass, 1987.

Angelo, T. A., and Cross, K. P. *Classroom Assessment Techniques: A Handbook for College Teachers.* (2nd ed.) San Francisco: Jossey-Bass, 1993.

Arreola, R. A. *Developing a Comprehensive Faculty Evaluation System.* Bolton, Mass.: Anker, 1994.

Bethany, B. H. "Instructional Systems Design." In R. Gagné (ed.), *Instructional Technology: Foundations.* Mahwah, N.J.: Erlbaum, 1987.

Bloom, B. S., Englehart, M. D., Furst, E. J., Hill, W. H., and Krathwohl, D. R. *Taxonomy of Educational Objectives: The Classification of Educational Goals. Handbook I: Cognitive Domain.* New York: McKay, 1956.

Boice, R. "Quick Starters: New Faculty Who Succeed." In M. Theall and J. Franklin (eds.), *Effective Practices for Improving Teaching.* New Directions for Teaching and Learning, no. 48. San Francisco: Jossey-Bass, 1991.

Boice, R. *The New Faculty Member: Supporting and Fostering Professional Development.* San Francisco: Jossey-Bass, 1992.

Boyer, E. L. *Scholarship Reconsidered: Priorities of the Professoriate.* Princeton, N.J.: Carnegie Foundation for the Advancement of Teaching, 1990.

Braskamp, L. A. "Connecting Research with Reality or Connecting Research with Practice: A Challenge." Paper presented at the Eightieth Annual Meeting of the American Educational Research Association, Montreal, Apr. 22, 1999.

Brinko, K. T., and Menges, R. J. *Practically Speaking: A Source Book for Instructional Consultants in Higher Education.* Stillwater, Okla.: New Forums Press, 1997.

Cashin, W. E. "Students Do Rate Different Academic Fields Differently." In M. Theall and J. Franklin (eds.), *Student Ratings of Instruction: Issues for Improving Practice.* New Directions for Teaching and Learning, no. 43. San Francisco: Jossey-Bass, 1990.

Centra, J. A., *Determining Faculty Effectiveness: Assessing Teaching, Research, and Service for Personnel Decisions and Improvement.* San Francisco: Jossey-Bass, 1979.

Centra, J. A., and Gaubatz, N. B. "Is There Gender Bias in Student Ratings of Instruction?" Paper presented at the Seventy-Ninth Annual Meeting of the American Educational Research Association, San Diego, Calif., Apr. 14, 1998.

Chickering, A. W., and Gamson, Z. F. "Seven Principles for Good Practice in Undergraduate Education." *AAHE Bulletin*, 1987, *39*(7), 3–7.

Chickering, A. W., and Gamson, Z. F. *Applying the Seven Principles for Good Practice in Undergraduate Education.* New Directions for Teaching and Learning, no. 47. San Francisco: Jossey-Bass, 1991.

Chiu, S., Wardrop, J. L., and Ryan, K. E. "Use of the Unbalanced Nested ANOVA to Examine the Relationship of Class Size to Student Ratings of Instructional Quality." Paper presented at the Eightieth Annual Meeting of the American Educational Research Association, Montreal, Apr. 22, 1999.

Chu, G. C., and Schramm, W. *Learning from Television: What the Research Says.* Washington, D.C.: National Association of Educational Broadcasters, 1967.

Clark, D. J., and Bekey, J. "Use of Small Groups in Instructional Evaluation." *Insight into Teaching Excellence,* 1979, *7*(1), 2–5.

Clark, R. E. "Reconsidering Research on Learning from Media." *Review of Educational Research,* 1983, *53*(4), 445–459.

Cohen, P. A. "Student Ratings of Instruction and Student Achievement: A Meta-Analysis of Multisection Validity Studies." *Review of Educational Research,* 1981, *31*(3), 281–309.

Crittenden, K. S., and Norr, J. L. "Student Values and Teacher Evaluation: A Problem in Person Perception." *Sociometry,* 1973, *36*(2), 143–151.

Cronbach, L. J., and Snow, R. E. *Individual Differences in Learning Ability as a Function of Instructional Variables.* Washington, D.C.: Office of Education, U.S. Department of Health, Education, and Welfare, 1969.

Cross, K. P., and Angelo, T. A. *Classroom Assessment Techniques: A Handbook for Faculty.* Ann Arbor, Mich.: National Center for Research to Improve Postsecondary Teaching and Learning, 1988.

Davis, B. G. *Tools for Teaching.* San Francisco: Jossey-Bass, 1993.

Diamond, R. M. *Designing and Improving Courses and Curricula in Higher Education: A Systematic Approach.* San Francisco: Jossey-Bass, 1989.

Doyle, K. O. *Evaluating Teaching.* San Francisco: New Lexington Press, 1983.

Farmer, D. W. "Institutional Improvement and Motivated Faculty." In M. Theall (ed.), *Motivation from Within: Encouraging Faculty and Students to Excel.* New Directions for Teaching and Learning, no. 78. San Francisco: Jossey-Bass, 1999.

Feldman, K. A. "The Association Between Student Ratings of Specific Instructional Dimensions and Student Achievement: Refining and Extending the Synthesis of Data from Multisection Validity Studies." *Research in Higher Education,* 1989, *30*(6), 583–645.

Feldman, K. A. "College Students' Views of Male and Female College Teachers. Part 1: Evidence from the Social Laboratory and Experiments." *Research in Higher Education,* 1992a, *33*(3), 317–375.

Feldman, K. A. "College Students' Views of Male and Female College Teachers. Part 2: Evidence from Students' Evaluations of Their Classroom Teachers." *Research in Higher Education,* 1992b, *33*(4), 415–474.

Feldman, K. A., and Paulsen, M. B. *Teaching and Learning in the College Classroom.* Needham Heights, Mass.: Ginn, 1998.

Feldman, K. A., and Paulsen, M. B. "Faculty Motivation: The Role of a Supportive Teaching Culture." In M. Theall (ed.), *Motivation from Within: Encouraging Faculty and Students to Excel.* New Directions for Teaching and Learning, no. 78. San Francisco: Jossey-Bass, 1999.

Forsyth, D. R., and McMillan, J. H. "Practical Proposals for Motivating Students." In R. J. Menges and M. D. Svinicki (eds.), *College Teaching: From Theory to Practice.* New Directions for Teaching and Learning, no. 45. San Francisco: Jossey-Bass, 1991.

Franklin, J., and Theall, M. "Who Reads Ratings: Knowledge, Attitudes, and Practices of Users of Student Ratings of Instruction." Paper presented at the Seventieth Annual Meeting of the American Educational Research Association, San Francisco, Mar. 31, 1989. (ED 306 241)

Franklin, J., and Theall, M. "Grade Inflation and Student Ratings: A Closer Look." Paper presented at the Seventy-Second Annual Meeting of the American Educational Research Association, Chicago, Apr. 7, 1991. (ED 349 318)

Franklin, J., and Theall, M. "Disciplinary Differences, Instructional Goals and Activities, Measures of Student Performance, and Student Ratings of Instruction." Paper presented at the Seventy-Third Annual Meeting of the American Educational Research Association, San Francisco, Apr. 22, 1992.

Franklin, J., and Theall, M. "Student Ratings of Instruction and Sex Differences Revisited." Paper presented at the Seventy-Fifth Annual Meeting of the American Educational Research Association, New Orleans, Apr. 7, 1994.

Gibbons, J. F., Kincheloe, W. R., and Down, K. S. "Tutored Videotape Instruction: A New Use of Electronics Media in Education." *Science,* March 1977, V195, 1138–1145.

Gillmore, G. M., Greenwald, A. G., Abrami, P. C., D'Apollonia, S., Marsh, H. W., and Roche, L. Debate presented at the Seventy-Ninth Annual Meeting of the American Educational Research Association, San Diego, Apr. 17, 1998.

Grasha, A. F. *Teaching with Style.* Pittsburgh, Pa.: Alliance Press, 1996.

Greenwald, A, G., and Gillmore, G. M. "Grading Leniency Is a Removable Contaminant of Student Ratings." *American Psychologist,* 1997a, 52(11), 1209–1217.

Greenwald, A, G., and Gillmore, G. M. "No Pain, No Gain? The Importance of Measuring Course Workload in Student Ratings of Instruction." *Journal of Educational Psychology,* 1997b, 89(4), 743–751.

Hardy, N. T. "A Survey Designed to Refine an Inventory of Teaching Styles to Be Used by Individuals Preparing for College Teaching." Unpublished doctoral dissertation, Michigan State University, 1976.

Hativa, N. "Expert University Teachers: Thinking, Knowledge, and Practice Regarding Effective Teaching Behaviors." Paper presented at the Eightieth Annual Meeting of the American Educational Research Association, Montreal, Apr. 23, 1999a.

Hativa, N. "Toward a Conceptual Framework of Dimensions of Effective Instruction: The Role of High-, Intermediate-, and Low-Inference Teaching Behaviors." *Instructional Evaluation and Faculty Development,* 1999b, 19(1), 3–12.

Haugen, L. *Writing a Teaching Philosophy Statement.* Ames: Iowa State University, 1998.

Holland, J. L. *Making Vocational Choices.* (2nd ed.) Upper Saddle River, N.J.: Prentice Hall, 1985.

Johnson, D. W., Johnson, R. T., and Smith, K. A. *Cooperative Learning: Increasing College Faculty Productivity.* ASHE-ERIC Higher Education Report, no. 4. Washington, D.C.: George Washington University, 1991.

Johnson, R. T., and Johnson, D. W. *Cooperation and Competition Theory and Research.* Edina, Minn.: Interaction, 1989.

Keller, J. M. "Development and Use of the ARCS Model of Instructional Design." *Journal of Instructional Development,* 1987, 10(3), 2–10.

Kolb, D. A. *Experiential Learning: Experience as the Source of Learning and Development.* Upper Saddle River, N.J.: Prentice Hall, 1984.

Krathwohl, D. R., Bloom, B. S., and Masia, B. B. *Taxonomy of Educational Objectives: The Classification of Educational Goals. Handbook II: Affective Domain.* New York: McKay, 1956.

Kulik, C. C., Kulik, J. A., and Cohen, P. A. "Instructional Technology and College Teaching." *Teaching of Psychology,* 1980, 7(4), 199–205.

Lowman, J. *Mastering the Techniques of Teaching.* San Francisco: Jossey-Bass, 1984.

Machell, D. F. "A Discourse on Professorial Melancholia." *Community Review,* 1989, 9(1–2), 41–50.

Marsh, H. W. "Student Evaluations of University Teaching: Research Findings, Methodological Issues, and Directions for Future Research." *International Journal of Educational Research*, 1987, *11*, 253–388.

Marsh, H. W., and Hocevar, D. "The Factorial Invariance of Student Evaluations of College Teaching." *American Educational Research Journal*, 1984, *21*(2), 341–366.

McKeachie, W. J. "Connecting Teaching to Learning." Address presented at the University of Illinois, Springfield, Mar. 3, 1999a.

McKeachie, W. J. *Teaching Tips: Strategies, Research, and Theory for College and University Teachers*. (10th ed.) Boston: Houghton Mifflin, 1999b.

McKinnon, M. M. "Core Elements of Student Motivation in Problem-Based Learning." In M. Theall (ed.), *Motivation from Within: Encouraging Faculty and Students to Excel.* New Directions for Teaching and Learning, no. 78. San Francisco: Jossey-Bass, 1999.

Menec, V. H., Perry, R. P., Struthers, C. W., Schonwetter, D. J., Hechter, F. J., and Eichholz, B. L. "Assisting At-Risk College Students with Attributional Retraining and Effective Teaching." *Journal of Applied Social Psychology*, 1994, *24*(8), 675–701.

Menges, R. J., and Mathis, B. C. *Key Resources on Teaching, Learning, Curriculum, and Faculty Development: A Guide to Higher Education Literature*. San Francisco: Jossey-Bass, 1988.

Mielke, K. "Asking the Right ETV Questions." *Educational Broadcasting Review*, 1968, *2*(6), 54–61.

Miller, R. I. *Evaluating Faculty for Promotion and Tenure*. San Francisco: Jossey-Bass, 1987.

Murray, H. "Low-Inference Classroom Teaching Behaviors and Student Ratings of College Teaching Effectiveness." *Journal of Educational Psychology*, 1983, *75*(1), 138–149.

Murray, H. "Effective Teaching Behaviors in the College Classroom." In J. C. Smart (ed.), *Higher Education Handbook of Theory and Research*. Vol. 7. New York: Agathon, 1991.

Myers, I. B. *Gifts Differing*. Palo Alto, Calif.: Consulting Psychologists Press, 1990.

Palmer, P. J. *To Know as We Are Known: Education as a Spiritual Journey*. New York: HarperCollins, 1983.

Palmer, P. J. *The Courage to Teach: Exploring the Inner Landscape of a Teacher's Life*. San Francisco: Jossey-Bass, 1997.

Panitz, T. "Benefits of Cooperation in Relation to Student Motivation." In M. Theall (ed.), *Motivation from Within: Encouraging Faculty and Students to Excel.* New Directions for Teaching and Learning, no. 78. San Francisco: Jossey-Bass, 1999.

Pascarella, E. T., and Terenzini, P. T. *How College Affects Students: Findings and Insights from Twenty Years of Research*. San Francisco: Jossey-Bass, 1991.

Paulsen, M. B., and Feldman, K. A. "Student Motivation and Epistemological Beliefs." In M. Theall (ed.), *Motivation from Within: Approaches for Encouraging Faculty and Students to Excel.* New Directions for Teaching and Learning, no. 78. San Francisco: Jossey-Bass, 1999.

Perry, R. P. "Perceived Control in the College Classroom." In J. C. Smart (ed.), *Higher Education Handbook of Theory and Research*. Vol. 7. New York: Agathon, 1991.

Pescosolido, B. A., and Aminzade, R. *The Social Worlds of Higher Education: Handbook for Teaching in a New Century*. Thousand Oaks, Calif.: Pine Forge Press, 1999.

Pintrich, P. R. (ed.). *Understanding Self-Regulated Learning*. New Directions for Teaching and Learning, no. 63. San Francisco: Jossey-Bass, 1995.

Pintrich, P. R., McKeachie, W. J., Smith, D.A.F., Doljanac, R., Lin, Y., Naveh-Benjamin, M., Crooks, T., and Karabenick, S. *Motivated Strategies for Learning Questionnaire*. (rev. ed.) Ann Arbor, Mich.: National Center for Research to Improve Postsecondary Teaching and Learning, 1988.

Reigeluth, C. M. *Instructional Design Theories and Models*. Mahwah, N.J.: Erlbaum, 1983.

Russell, T. L. *The No Significant Difference Phenomenon*. Raleigh: North Carolina State University, 1999.

Salomon, G. A. *Interaction of Media, Cognition, and Learning.* San Francisco: Jossey-Bass, 1969.

Schön, D. A. *The Reflective Practitioner.* New York: Basic Books, 1983.

Schön, D. A. *Educating the Reflective Practitioner: Toward a New Design for Teaching and Learning in the Professions.* San Francisco: Jossey-Bass, 1991.

Scriven, M. "The Methodology of Evaluation." In R. Tyler, R. Gagné, and M. Scriven (eds.), *Perspectives of Curriculum Evaluation.* Skokie, Ill.: Rand McNally, 1967.

Seldin, P., and Associates. *The Teaching Portfolio.* Boston, Mass.: Anker, 1991.

Shore, B. M., Foster, S. F., Knapper, C. K., Nadeau, G. G., Neill, N., and Sim, V. W. *The Teaching Dossier: A Guide to Its Preparation and Use.* Ottawa: Canadian Association of University Professors, 1986.

Shulman, L. S. "Those Who Understand: Knowledge Growth in Teaching." *Educational Researcher,* 1986, *15*(2), 4–14.

Shulman, L. S. "Knowledge and Teaching: Foundations of the New Reform." *Harvard Educational Review,* 1987, *57*(1), 1–22.

Shulman, L. S. "Toward a Pedagogy of Substance." *AAHE Bulletin,* 1989, *41*(10), 8–13.

Smart, J. C., and Feldman, K. A. "Accentuation Effects of Dissimilar Academic Departments: An Application and Exploration of Holland's Theory." *Research in Higher Education,* 1998, *39*(4), 385–418.

Stark, J. S., Lowther, M. A., Ryan, M. P., Bomotti, S. S., Haven, G. L., and Martens, G. *Reflections on Course Planning: Faculty and Students Consider Influences and Goals.* Ann Arbor, Mich.: National Center for Research to Improve Postsecondary Education, 1988.

Svinicki, M. D., and Dixon, N. M. "The Kolb Model Modified for Classroom Activities." *College Teaching,* 1987, *35*(4), 141–146.

Theall, M., Birdsall, M., and Franklin, J. "Motivating Students: A Practical Guide for Teachers." Unpublished monograph available in draft form at [www.uis.edu/~ctl/motive.html], 1997.

Theall, M., and Franklin, J. (eds.). *Student Ratings of Instruction: Issues for Improving Practice.* New Directions for Teaching and Learning, no. 43. San Francisco: Jossey-Bass, 1990.

Theall, M., and Franklin, J. (eds.). *Effective Practices for Improving Teaching.* New Directions for Teaching and Learning, no. 48. San Francisco: Jossey-Bass, 1991.

Wilson, R. C. "Improving Faculty Teaching: Effective Use of Student Evaluations and Consultants." *Journal of Higher Education,* 1986, *57*(2), 196–211.

MICHAEL THEALL *is associate professor of educational administration and director of the Center for Teaching and Learning at the University of Illinois, Springfield.*

PART TWO

A Reprise of Popular Topics: Where Are They Now?

3

Issue 14, Learning in Groups, *featured one of the earliest discussions of what has since become the collaborative method. Here one of the original authors traces the development of this burgeoning field.*

Group-Based Learning

Russell Y. Garth

Nearly seventeen years ago, Clark Bouton and I convened a group of individuals who were making at least some use of group-based pedagogical approaches in their classrooms—practices now typically known as collaborative or cooperative learning. One result of that meeting was *Learning in Groups,* volume 14 in the *New Directions for Teaching and Learning* series. Reflecting on that publication, I was curious about three things. What does volume 14 suggest about the entire *New Directions* series? Did that volume have any particular influence on the series? And how has its topic, collaborative and cooperative learning, evolved since then?

Ideas from Practice

In 1982, I was a program officer at the U.S. Department of Education's Fund for the Improvement of Postsecondary Education (FIPSE). Those of us on the staff believed, with doctrinal fervor but limited proof, that the best ideas for improving postsecondary education came from practice rather than from research and development (R&D) models. We thought that experiments arising from and working with the messiness of the world were the ones most likely to solve actual problems and thus be continued by the institution. We worried that cleaner R&D approaches, which were used in a number of government programs, might be inevitable in designing expensive stealth bombers but unlikely to be sufficiently nuanced to survive the realities of human systems such as colleges. My sense now is that the actual educational approaches have been coming from practice rather than research, but the research on learning is providing a deeper knowledge of why these educational approaches seemed to have been working, which is perhaps one of the hallmarks of the *New Directions* series.

One of our challenges, therefore, was to be able to spot patterns of improvement among these various real-life projects, lift up underlying ideas for scrutiny, shape those ideas so that others might find them useful, and then share the ideas widely. The result, we envisioned, would be ideas more general than dissemination materials from a single institution but less elaborate and abstract than academic theories—the kinds of ideas, in short, that could inspire and empower others to greater success as they tackled similar problems on their own campuses.

At FIPSE, we tested our notions about ideas from practice in various ways (a subject for another time), but the *New Directions* series had always struck me as one directly relevant approach. Then and since I have affectionately referred to *New Directions* volumes as "quick and dirty." Of modest length, with multiple authors, built-in editing and production, and an existing marketing apparatus, they are tailor-made for developing ideas—out of dirty practice—fairly quickly. This notion of ideas from practice was part of the impetus for *Learning in Groups* and still seems one good way to view this series and to answer my first question about what sort of publication—and series—this is.

The Far End of the Bookshelf

It is then appropriate to ask the second question, whether the *Learning in Groups* volume made any difference, because influence is the actual test of the ideas-from-practice argument just made. The answer is that there is reason to think it did have an effect.

When we put the volume together, the idea of using groups as a critical strategy for enhancing student learning was not novel, but it was also not prevalent. And perhaps most significant, few analysts truly understood the educational power of student-to-student collaboration. In the intervening seventeen years, this understanding has spread and deepened; I will comment on that development shortly. But in thinking about the influence of a particular publication, it is important to know whether the overall field is in ascendancy or in decline. In this case, collaborative and cooperative learning seems to have continued to grow, even attaining status as something of a movement.

The volume itself came out of a group of projects supported by FIPSE. As we said in the Editors' Notes at the time:

> Interestingly, the use of learning groups was often not seen by teachers as the basic description of what they were doing, since learning groups were usually only part of a larger instructional strategy. These teachers were trying to teach writing, improve medical practice in rural areas, or encourage faculty to think more seriously about the nature of their teaching. They saw themselves as using problem-solving techniques, as putting the learner first, or as making the student think. They were all using learning groups, but they did not all see that that was the key to the success that they were having.

Indeed, group-based learning was only loosely recognized as a topic. The FIPSE guidelines in those years included *learning groups* along with experiential learning, individualized learning, and interactive technologies under a general rubric of *active learning* (which was not a very common term at that time either). There was not much writing about using groups to enhance learning, at least of a general, nondisciplinary character, so there was scant foundation for collective conceptual work. A few of the individuals contributing to the volume knew of the work of M.L.J. Abercrombie in Great Britain, and several others were aware of the efforts of the Johnson brothers at the University of Minnesota, who had written at that point largely about the considerable body of practice and research on cooperative learning in K–12 education. As I recall, there were some shared general notions, stemming from such thinkers as John Dewey, Kurt Lewin, and Jean Piaget. But the intriguing surprise (because it was completely unfamiliar to me) was the fact that many of the contributors, who had not known each other, knew of the Russian psychologist L. S. Vygotsky and his concepts such as "zone of proximal development."

Zelda Gamson, using personal retrospective as a way of surveying the state of collaborative learning for a 1994 conference convened by the federally funded National Center on Postsecondary Teaching and Learning, noted that in the early 1980s we "did not have a name for these practices" (Kadel and Keehner, 1994). In that particular address, she specifically referred to *Learning in Groups* as "groundbreaking." And perhaps explaining that comment, she had once mentioned to me that publication of *Learning in Groups* encouraged her, Arthur Chickering, and their colleagues who were developing the Seven Principles for Good Practice in Undergraduate Education about that time to include "student collaboration" as one of the seven principles. The seven principles, I think, helped legitimize group-based learning as a key way to foster that collaboration.

Another critical element in moving these group-based pedagogies to a wider stage was the Collaboration in Undergraduate Education (CUE) action community sponsored by the American Association for Higher Education (AAHE). Also spearheaded by some FIPSE project directors, CUE provided an annual convention for educators using these approaches and a newsletter. It also typically sparked several sessions on the AAHE National Conference program.

It is possible, therefore, to see *Learning in Groups* as one of several pieces—along with individual practitioners, FIPSE funding, the seven principles, and CUE—that provided a platform of concepts, contacts, and credibility to a nascent movement.

In the early 1990s, this work assumed greater shape and richness as several national initiatives attempted to organize the growing body of practice and material. In 1992, the Collaborative Learning Project at Lesley College published *Collaboration in Undergraduate Education, Models II*, including a bibliography and descriptions of model programs with contact information (Tarule and Landa). In 1992 and 1994, the National Center on

Postsecondary Teaching and Learning (NCPTLA), federally funded and headquartered at Pennsylvania State University, culled existing material for the two volumes of *Collaborative Learning: A Sourcebook for Higher Education* (Goodsell and others, 1992; Kadel and Keehner, 1994). Jim Cooper and several colleagues from the Network for Cooperative Learning in Higher Education compiled three bibliographies on cooperative or collaborative learning (Cooper and Mueck, 1989; Cooper, McKinney, and Robinson, 1992; Cooper and Robinson, 1995).

In the Lesley College and NCTLA collections, *Learning in Groups* is the earliest work cited, and it is one of the earliest in Cooper and Mueck's 1989 bibliography. In addition, volume 1 of the two sourcebooks published by NCTLA reprinted one chapter from *Learning in Groups* ("Teachers and Learning Groups: Dissolution of the Atlas Complex" by Donald L. Finkel and G. Stephen Monk), a piece that current leaders in the field tell me has become a classic description of collaborative learning from the point of view of a faculty member.

Reviewing these, I began to picture our slim volume residing at the far end of a chronologically arranged bookshelf, pleased that it had not been summarily discarded shortly after publication and wondering whether it represented a kind of reference point, used to mark the beginning of a movement intentionally seeking definition and place.

More Conversations

I can still remember one of my own private parlor games dating from the period of developing *Learning in Groups:* If I could be granted one wish to improve learning in higher education, what would it be? At that time, I wished for more students to be engaged in more conversations, and revisiting that question now, I think that more conversations is still a plausible choice. For me, conversation is a kind of pedagogical shorthand, locating the source of learning not so much in the text or the ideas themselves or the professor or the student or even the professor-student relationship as in the student-to-student interaction about the ideas. Even though the body of writing, research, and practice about collaborative and cooperative learning has grown steadily in reach and sophistication, the central image of learners conversing with other learners about ideas remains at the core of this concept.

To address my third question about what has happened to these forms of group-based learning, we would then like to know whether there are more conversations going on now in higher education than in 1983.

In general, it seems that collaborative and cooperative learning are still on the upswing. A 1995 survey of college faculty conducted by the Higher Education Research Institute at the University of California in Los Angeles revealed that the top two teaching methods used in all or most courses were "cooperative learning" and "group projects," which also showed ratings increases of 9 percent and 7 percent, respectively, over six years earlier (Millis and Cottell, 1997).

Publications (now including electronic versions) are certainly another indicator. During the 1990s, the still growing quantity of articles has been joined by a handful of books (Bosworth and Hamilton, 1994; Bruffee, 1993, currently undergoing revision; Johnson, Johnson, and Smith, 1991; Millis and Cottell, 1997). Recently, the National Institute for Science Education has sponsored a first-rate Web site (www.wcer.wisc.edu/nise/CL1) on cooperative learning in math, sciences, and engineering that offers both how-to advice and numerous referrals to other writings. Indeed, another sign of energy was the movement's own internecine war—proponents of cooperative learning versus advocates for collaborative learning—played out, in part, in the pages of *Change* magazine (Bruffee, 1995; Matthews, Cooper, Davidson, and Hawkes, 1995).

To confirm my general sense of continued growth, especially because I had been somewhat detached from the richness of this ongoing work, I called seven leaders in this movement, seeking both broad overviews and some of the subtle dynamics of change. I detected an interesting paradox. Several individuals—perhaps a bit wistful for the early 1990s efforts to consolidate and raise the visibility of collaborative and cooperative learning—missed the presence of a single organization or recognized group to promote this issue. Yet all were encouraged by the considerable efforts of a range of disciplinary societies (accounting, writing, medicine, math, engineering, and natural sciences, among others) to promote these approaches via sourcebooks, Web sites, conference presentations, and affinity groups. And whatever passion might have once existed for cooperative versus collaborative bragging rights or turf fights seems largely spent, creating thereby a much more encompassing set of classroom strategies at everyone's disposal.

The diffusion of innovations throughout social institutions follows somewhat mysterious paths, and part of what might be simultaneously inspiriting and worrisome to those shaping this field of group-based strategies could be that these paths have become even less clearly marked over the past decade. Recently, I spent parts of three days with a working group of eight chief academic officers at the Council of Independent Colleges' annual Deans' Institute. At the end of that time, they held their own parlor game: What educational approaches, if more widely used on their campuses, could significantly enhance student learning? They came up with a package of five: collaborative learning, student portfolios, electronic communication, integrative experiences, and experiential learning. Not only is collaborative learning specifically included, but it is also complementary to—and in many cases essential to—these other educational approaches. This convergence is equally relevant in other currently discussed strategies such as problem-based or case-based learning.

Educators using and writing about group-based learning have, over the past seventeen years, fleshed out these approaches with a fertile repertoire of classroom technique, pedagogical strategy, impact assessment, and even suggestive revised perspectives on such deep-structure educational issues as authority relationships among subject, teacher, and learner. This work has in turn been bolstered by the new understandings of cognition emerging from psychological and neurological research. With a possible convergence of nonlecture teaching approaches, collaborative and cooperative learning may appear less frequently on signposts of beautiful but narrow roadways and more often as fellow travelers in a broad-bandwidth world leading toward enhanced learning.

References

Bosworth, K., and Hamilton, S. J. *Collaborative Learning: Underlying Processes and Effective Techniques.* New Directions for Teaching and Learning, no. 59. San Francisco: Jossey-Bass, 1994.

Bruffee, K. A. *Collaborative Learning, Higher Education, Interdependence, and the Authority of Knowledge.* Baltimore: Johns Hopkins University Press, 1993.

Bruffee, K. A. "Sharing Our Toys: Cooperative Versus Collaborative Learning." *Change,* Jan.-Feb. 1995, pp. 12–18.

Cooper, J., McKinney, M., and Robinson, P. "Cooperative/Collaborative Learning: Part II." *Journal of Staff, Program and Organizational Development,* 1992, 9, 240–252.

Cooper, J., and Mueck, R. "Annotated Bibliography of Cooperative/Collaborative Learning Research and Practice (Primarily) at the College Level." *Journal of Staff, Program and Organizational Development,* 1989, 7, 143–148.

Cooper, J., and Robinson, P. *An Annotated Bibliography of Cooperative Learning in Higher Education. Part III: The 1990s.* Stillwater, Okla.: New Forums Press, 1995.

Goodsell, A. S., Maher, M. R., Tinto, V., Smith, B. L., and MacGregor, J. *Collaborative Learning: A Sourcebook for Higher Education.* Vol. 1. University Park, Pa.: National Center on Postsecondary Teaching, Learning, and Assessment, 1992.

Johnson, D. W., Johnson, R. T., and Smith, K. A. *Cooperative Learning: Increasing College Faculty Instructional Productivity.* ASHE-ERIC Higher Education Report no. 4. Washington, D.C.: George Washington University, 1991.

Kadel, S., and Keehner, J. A. *Collaborative Learning: A Sourcebook for Higher Education.* Vol. 2. University Park, Pa.: National Center on Postsecondary Teaching, Learning, and Assessment, 1994.

Matthews, R. S., Cooper, J. L., Davidson, N., and Hawkes, P. "Building Bridges Between Cooperative and Collaborative Learning." *Change,* July-Aug. 1995, pp. 35–39.

Millis, B. J., and Cottell, P. G., Jr. *Cooperative Learning for Higher Education Faculty.* Phoenix: American Council on Education/Oryx Press, 1997.

Tarule, J. M., and Landa, A. *Collaboration in Undergraduate Education, Models II.* Cambridge, Mass.: Lesley College, 1992.

RUSSELL Y. GARTH, formerly program officer and acting deputy director of the Fund for the Improvement of Postsecondary Education (FIPSE), is currently executive vice president of the Council of Independent Colleges.

4

*Can we teach without communicating? Of course not.
But further, it is impossible to communicate with students
without honoring the centrality of the teacher-student
relationship.*

Can We Teach
Without Communicating?

Jean M. Civikly-Powell

When Kenneth Eble visited the University of New Mexico in the mid-1980s, I was fortunate to spend time with him and share my work in communication as it relates to teaching, including training the university's teaching assistants. My view of much of Eble's work, then and now, was through communication eyes, for how can we possibly teach without communicating? To my surprise, the *New Directions for Teaching and Learning* series had not addressed this teaching-communicating lifeline. I proposed the topic to Ken, editor-in-chief of the series at the time, and soon thereafter *Communicating in College Classrooms* became volume 26 in the series (Civikly, 1986).

Looking Back: Then and Since Then

What can scholars in the discipline of communication offer to the scholarship of teaching? *Communicating in College Classrooms* included chapters on the cultural dynamics of the teacher-student relationship, interpersonal communication, nonverbal communication, communication apprehension, authentic communication—teaching as loving, humor, communicator style, and teacher-student conflicts, all still vibrant areas of study in the field of instructional communication.

Teacher-Student Relationship. Reflecting on these topics, I have attempted to offer a thematic current. Clearly, *relationship* is the essential element. It takes two (at least) to communicate, to teach, to be included and excluded, to empathize, to argue, to encourage and to be clear (Civikly, 1992a, 1992b). Attention to the chapters on teaching as loving, interpersonal communication, humor, conflict, culture, and communication apprehension will serve to illustrate the centrality of the teacher-student relationship. Furthermore, Joel Jones's chapter, "The Art of Teaching: An Act of Love" (1986), serves well as the foundation for this discussion and my own sense of teaching. In my reflections on Jones's chapter, I see his essay as a forerunner of more recent works, best represented by bell hooks (1994), Maxine Greene (1995), and Parker Palmer (1997a). Jones's four teaching tenets—the self transcends technique, authenticity precedes authority, vulnerability precludes venerability, and less posture allows more person—have stood the test of time. His mind-set has been felt, heard, and endorsed by other educators:

"As I teach, I project the condition of my soul onto my students, my subject and our way of being together" (Palmer, 1997b, p. 15).

"Who we are is as important to our teaching as what we teach and how we teach it. . . . Rarely do we take the occasion, or find ourselves encouraged, to consider the individual qualities that we bring to our exacting endeavors" (Banner and Cannon, 1997, p. 42).

Hooks (1994) also speaks to the centrality of the person and the passion of teaching; two of her chapter titles reflect this: "Eros, Eroticism, and the Pedagogical Process" and "Ecstasy: Teaching and Learning Without Limits." In a critique of thirteen narratives about teaching, Sprague (1993) addressed the transformative power of communication and of the teacher-student relationship. She noted that "in the context of these thirteen stories that so fully document the individualized engagement of *good teaching*, it is hard to ignore the intimacy and even the sensuality that inheres in our work" (p. 362). Indeed, caring is a *relationship* and not just a personal attribute (Noddings, 1992). Noddings contends that in a caring relationship, a response is necessary to maintain the connection and that something as simple as a student's returned eye gaze is often sufficient to invigorate and nourish the teacher. Beidler and Tong (1991) discuss love in the classroom and encourage teachers "to teach responsibly, teach beautifully, yet also take the risks we must take to do full-blooded, bold, honest, loving teaching . . . to at all costs avoid that neutered, bloodless, embalmed, 'safe' kind of teaching" (p. 61).

In a study of teacher caring, Teven and McCroskey (1997) defined caring as having three dimensions: empathy, understanding, and responsiveness. They found that students who perceive their teachers as caring about them evaluated the teacher and the course content more positively and reported that they learned more in the course. Teven and McCroskey suggest that a teacher's positive nonverbal behaviors ("immediacy") may be what is cuing the students' perceptions of teacher caring.

According to both personal accounts and empirical studies, the pulse of the teacher's personhood is deafening. "We need to open a new frontier in our exploration of good teaching: the inner landscape of a teacher's life.

To chart that landscape fully, three important paths must be taken—intellectual, emotional, and spiritual—and none can be ignored" (Palmer, 1997b, p. 15).

Immediacy. Since the 1986 volume *Communicating in College Classrooms,* a construct known as immediacy has gained prominence in the communication literature. Immediacy is defined as perceived closeness and support. It includes both verbal and nonverbal behaviors that signal accessibility, interest, and involvement. Verbal immediacy is demonstrated in expressions of unity ("we," "our") and statements of interest, liking, support, and encouragement. Nonverbal immediacy is evidenced by relaxed and pleasant facial expressions and gestures, smiling, leaning toward the student, socially appropriate touch and eye contact, vocal expressiveness, and interactive classroom seating. Research over the past twenty years provides strong positive correlations between teacher immediacy and effective teaching (Plax and Kearney, 1998; Christophel, 1990). Andersen and Andersen (1987) suggested that teachers can learn immediacy behaviors, provided they feel positively about their students.

Interpersonal Communication. Interpersonal communication in the teacher-student relationship threads the fabric of teaching and learning. Joseph De Vito's premise that teaching follows the stages of the development of a relationship (1986) continues to receive support today. In subsequent writing, De Vito (1990) presented a model of "teaching as interpersonal competence" and articulated ten communication skills essential to effective teaching: openness, empathy, supportiveness, positiveness, equality, confidence, immediacy, expressiveness, other-orientation, and interaction management. Examples for two of these skills illustrate the attention to the teacher-student relationship. The skill of openness involves a willingness to self-disclose, to admit to uncertainty, to give honest feedback, and to take responsibility for one's thoughts and feelings. Commenting on empathy, De Vito noted that empathic teachers are willing to feel the confusion, frustration, and interests, the highs and the lows, that the student feels. "Without empathy teaching becomes a one-way process, much more efficiently handled by even the most elementary software" (De Vito, 1990, p. 75).

Humor. Another relational communication experience is the teacher's use of humor. Though we have little evidence to suggest that humor is a *causal* agent in students' retention of information, students consistently report finding their classes a more enjoyable learning experience when humor is used. The conjecture about the role of humor in student learning is that humor helps promote greater student attention and comprehension, and if nothing else, "humor is a mental workout" (Civikly, 1992b, p. 137) that challenges the mind to discover why something is incongruous or funny.

Some developmental factors also appear to be involved in the use of humor in college teaching. Javidi and Long (1989) discovered that inexperienced teachers use less humor than experienced teachers. Their finding may be helpful to faculty who work with teaching assistants and other novice educators. Downs, Javidi, and Nussbaum (1988) found that teachers use humor more frequently in the early part of the semester, which may suggest that humor is serving as a teacher strategy for developing affinity in the teacher-student relationship.

Teacher immediacy is also a consideration when humor is used. Gorham and Christophel (1990) reported that the combination of teacher humor and immediacy behaviors increased the likelihood of student learning. They concluded that teachers with very low verbal and nonverbal immediacy may not benefit from increasing their proportion of positive humor unless they increase their use of other immediacy behaviors as well. They also cautioned that teachers with very high verbal and nonverbal immediacy might experience "overkill" if they continue to add to the number of stories they tell and exceed the students' "story threshold." As Darling and Civikly (1986) noted, without a positive relational base in which students feel safe and feel liked by the teacher, humor can be a risky teacher endeavor. Teacher humor that is not perceived as open, honest, relevant, and spontaneous may be more destructive to the communication climate of the class than an absence of humor.

Conflict. Another interpersonal phenomenon seen in classrooms, although usually not welcomed, is conflict. Recent communication research literature on conflict management has addressed issues of power in the classroom and the classroom dynamics of compliance seeking and compliance resistance. Faculty and teaching assistants report different experiences and concerns about management predicaments they face in their teaching (Civikly-Powell, 1996). Experienced teachers are more likely to use a variety of strategies for management of student misbehaviors. Plax and Kearney (1998) predict that "by engaging in nonverbal immediacy behaviors of approach, teachers will find their students to be more willing to comply and less willing to resist" (p. 282). Kearney, Plax, Hays, and Ivey (1991) have also examined *teacher* misbehaviors and suggested that students misbehave largely because their teachers do.

Joyce Hocker (1986) reflects on how changes in the past decade seem to affect the college classroom environment. The growing cohort of nontraditional students, for example, struggles with meeting their teacher's demands and meeting their own pressures about child care, family obligations, and conflicting work schedules and demands. Not surprisingly, stress intensifies in both students and teachers. Students who are receiving financial aid from their parents also experience added pressure to succeed, particularly as tuition costs escalate. Thus teacher-student confrontations may have "ghost parties" in the form of parents, spouses, employers, and children. Professors report more stress as they attempt to meet demands to teach larger classes, learn new technologies, and face shrinking budgets.

Socialization. An interpretation of culture, known as socialization, has gained prominence in the instructional communication research literature. Staton and Hunt (1992), Staton (1998), Darling (1998), and Cawyer and Friedrich (1998) have examined the role of communication and ways in which faculty and graduate teaching assistants (GTAs) learn their cultures, that is, the expectations and behaviors of their teaching roles and departmental environments. What is the nature of the verbal and nonverbal communication processes by which faculty and GTAs make sense of their teaching environments? "Teachers who enter the profession with a consistent, well-grounded understanding of the institutional context, themselves, and their teaching philosophy have a greater likelihood of enacting the role of teacher successfully. These factors interact to influence teachers' willingness to take instructional risks, reshape their views of students, influence their response to contextual constraints, and ultimately structure their enactment of the teacher role" (Staton and Hunt, 1992, p. 131).

Communication Apprehension. Of the topics discussed in the 1986 volume, communication apprehension has received the most empirical attention. Our society and our teachers continue to examine the fears of communicating in a variety of contexts and ways to lessen these fears. Review of almost any issue of the journal *Communication Education* can assist faculty in understanding the relationship between communication apprehension and such variables as learning style preference, nonverbal behaviors, immediacy, expectations, cognitive performance, listening comprehension, self-disclosure, positive thinking, decision making, and new communication technologies. Both teacher and student factors determine the extent to which students participate in class (Civikly, 1992b). This leads Kougl (1997) to pose an important question: "Is the student choosing to be silent, or does the silence control the student?" (p. 126).

Looking Ahead: What's Down the Road?

In the past decade, enormous technological changes have taken place that affect instructional communication (Daly, 1998) and may at times seem to threaten the teacher-student relationship. For example, how is the process of communication affected when that interaction occurs electronically? Are the textures of interpersonal communication and teacher-student interaction via computers different from face-to-face interactions? Is the fundamental process of communication altered when it occurs via computers? In what ways do people adapt their communication messages for electronic transmission? Specific applications relevant to these questions involve instruction in distance learning settings. How has e-mail changed the teacher-student relationship and student-student relationships? Have these relationships become more personal? Less personal? More task-focused? How has e-mail affected the globalization of teaching and learning? Do students and faculty with particular personalities or cultural backgrounds approach interactions more easily via e-mail communication than face to face?

And even with all these technological tools, the in-class face-to-face issues continue to confront and perplex teachers and students: the teacher-student relationship, class interactions, conflicts and conflict management, nonverbal messages, uses of humor, motivational strategies, compliance seeking, teacher credibility, and instructional clarity.

For each of these concerns, there is a communication component. For each of these concerns, communication scholars continue to study the classroom setting and the teacher-student relationship. For we cannot teach without communicating.

References

Andersen, J. F., and Andersen, P. A. "Never Smile Until Christmas? Casting Doubts on an Old Myth." *Journal of Thought,* 1987, 22(3), 57–61.

Banner, J. M., and Cannon, H. C. "The Personal Qualities of Teaching." *Change,* 1997, 29(6), 40–43.

Beidler, P. G., and Tong, R. "Love in the Classroom." *Journal of Excellence in College Teaching,* 1991, 2(X), 53–70.

Cawyer, C. S., and Friedrich, G. W. "Organizational Socialization: Processes for New Communication Faculty." *Communication Education,* 1998, 47(3), 234–245.

Christophel, D. M. "The Relationship Among Teacher Immediacy Behaviors, Student Motivation, and Learning." *Communication Education,* 1990, 39(4), 323–340.

Civikly, J. M. (ed.). *Communicating in College Classrooms.* New Directions for Teaching and Learning, no. 26. San Francisco: Jossey-Bass, 1986.

Civikly, J. M. "Clarity: Teachers and Students Making Sense of Instruction." *Communication Education,* 1992a, 41(2), 138–152.

Civikly, J. M. *Classroom Communication: Principles and Practice.* Dubuque, Iowa: Brown, 1992b.

Civikly-Powell, J. M. "Classroom Management Issues for Faculty and Teaching Assistants: Research Findings and Video Demonstrations." Paper presented at the Western States Communication Association Conference, San Diego, Feb. 1996.

Daly, J. A. "Distance Education." In A. L. Vangelisti, J. A. Daly, and G. W. Friedrich (eds.), *Teaching Communication.* (2nd ed.) Mahwah, N.J.: Erlbaum, 1998.

Darling, A. L. "Becoming a Professional." In A. L. Vangelisti, J. A. Daly, and G. W. Friedrich (eds.), *Teaching Communication.* (2nd ed.) Mahwah, N.J.: Erlbaum, 1998.

Darling, A. L., and Civikly, J. M. "The Effect of Teacher Humor on Student Perceptions of Classroom Communicative Climate." *Journal of Classroom Interaction,* 1986, 22(1), 24–30.

De Vito, J. A. "Teaching as Relationship Development." In J. M. Civikly (ed.), *Communicating in College Classrooms.* New Directions for Teaching and Learning, no. 26. San Francisco: Jossey-Bass, 1986.

De Vito, J. A. "Teaching Interpersonally." In R. A. Fiordo (ed.), *Communication in Education.* Calgary, Alberta, Canada: Detselig Enterprises, 1990.

Downs, V., Javidi, M. N., and Nussbaum, J. "An Analysis of Teachers' Verbal Communication Within the College Classroom: Use of Humor, Self-Disclosure, and Narratives." *Communication Education,* 1988, 37(2), 127–141.

Gorham, J., and Christophel, D. M. "The Relationship of Teachers' Use of Humor in the Classroom to Immediacy and Student Learning." *Communication Education,* 1990, 39(1), 46–62.

Greene, M. *Releasing the Imagination.* San Francisco: Jossey-Bass, 1995.

Hocker, J. L. "Teacher-Student Confrontations." In J. M. Civikly (ed.), *Communicating in College Classrooms.* New Directions for Teaching and Learning, no. 26. San Francisco: Jossey-Bass, 1986.

hooks, b. *Teaching to Transgress: Education as the Practice of Freedom.* New York: Routledge, 1994.

Javidi, M. N., and Long, L. W. "Teachers' Use of Humor, Self-Disclosure, and Narra-
tive Activity as a Function of Experience." *Communication Research Reports,* 1989,
6(1), 47–52.

Jones, J. M. "The Art of Teaching: An Act of Love." In J. M. Civikly (ed.), *Communicating in College Classrooms.* New Directions for Teaching and Learning, no. 26. San
Francisco: Jossey-Bass, 1986.

Kearney, P., Plax, T. G., Hays, E. R., and Ivey, M. J. "College Teacher Misbehaviors:
What Students Say They Don't Like About What Their Teachers Say and Do." *Communication Quarterly,* 1991, 39(4), 309–324.

Kougl, K. *Communicating in the Classroom.* Prospect Heights, Ill.: Waveland Press, 1997.

Noddings, N. *The Challenge to Care in Schools: An Alternative Approach to Education.* New
York: Teachers College Press, 1992.

Palmer, P. J. *The Courage to Teach: Exploring the Inner Landscape of a Teacher's Life.* San
Francisco: Jossey-Bass, 1997a.

Palmer, P. J. "The Heart of a Teacher: Identity and Integrity in Teaching." *Change,*
1997b, 29(6), 15–21.

Plax, T. G., and Kearney, P. "Classroom Management: Contending with College Student
Discipline." In A. L. Vangelisti, J. A. Daly, and G. W. Friedrich (eds.), *Teaching Communication.* (2nd ed.) Mahwah, N.J.: Erlbaum, 1998.

Sprague, J. "Why Teaching Works: The Transformative Power of Pedagogical Communication." *Communication Education,* 1993, 42(4), 349–366.

Staton, A. Q. "An Ecological Perspective on College/University Teaching: The Teaching/
Learning Environment and Socialization." In A. L. Vangelisti, J. A. Daly, and G. W.
Friedrich (eds.), *Teaching Communication.* (2nd ed.) Mahwah, N.J.: Erlbaum, 1998.

Staton, A. Q., and Hunt, S. L. "Teacher Socialization: Review and Conceptualization."
Communication Education, 1992, 41(2), 109–137.

Teven, J. J., and McCroskey, J. M. "The Relationship of Perceived Teacher Caring with
Student Learning and Teacher Evaluation." *Communication Education,* 1997, 46(1), 1–9.

*JEAN M. CIVIKLY-POWELL is a professor of communication at the University of
New Mexico and director of the university's Teaching Assistant Resource Center.*

5

*Changes in technology and the workplace have made the
ability to think critically more important than ever
before. Instruction designed to help college students think
critically focuses on skills that are widely applicable
across domains of knowledge and the disposition to use
these skills.*

Teaching for Critical Thinking:
Helping College Students Develop
the Skills and Dispositions
of a Critical Thinker

Diane F. Halpern

It is twenty years since Robert E. Young served as guest editor of the issue
of *New Directions for Teaching and Learning* titled *Fostering Critical Thinking* (1980) and thirteen years since James E. Stice accepted the same task in
the issue titled *Developing Critical Thinking and Problem-Solving Abilities*
(1987). These pioneers, including the authors of the chapters in these volumes, took us in a *new direction* in the early and mid-1980s, but where are
we now, at the start of the third millennium, in our efforts to help students
improve how they think? Young and Stice would be pleased to know that
we have made progress in achieving the goals they set for us and would not
be surprised to learn that we still have far to go.

The Naysayers Were (Mostly) Wrong

Many authorities in higher education did not enthusiastically embrace the
idea that college students should receive explicit instruction in how to
think. Not that the academic community was opposed to good thinking, but
many educators believed that it was a misguided effort. For example, Glaser
(1984) cited abundant evidence of critical thinking failures in support of his
argument that thinking skills are context-bound and do not transfer across
academic domains. Glaser and other skeptics were partly correct. Better
thinking is not a necessary outcome of traditional, discipline-based instruction. However, when thinking skills are explicitly taught for transfer, using

 69

multiple examples from several disciplines, students can learn to improve how they think in ways that transfer across academic domains. Rubinstein's highly successful course in problem solving (Rubinstein and Firstenberg, 1987), Lochhead and Whimby's analytical reasoning procedures (1987), and Woods's use of deliberate planning and monitoring (1987), all of which were described in Stice's volume, provided models of successful instruction in critical thinking that eventually swayed even the staunchest critics.

Many colleges and universities in North America now offer courses specifically designed to enhance their students' abilities to think critically, as part of the general education requirements. In fact, critical thinking instruction briefly assumed center stage on our national education agenda when the commission that wrote educational goals for the United States for the year 2000 established the following goal: "The proportion of college graduates who demonstrate an advanced ability to think critically, communicate effectively, and solve problems will increase substantially" (National Education Goals Panel, 1991, p. 62). Although support for the development of college-level thinking skills was a nonpartisan issue, with backing from both the Bush and Clinton administrations, no funding was ever provided to make this goal a reality. Nevertheless, dedicated professors and concerned community leaders have continued to define the enhancement of critical thinking as a primary reason for higher education.

Definitions and Assumptions

Young began his edited volume on critical thinking by asking, "Critical thinking: What is it?" (1980, p. viii). Although a variety of definitions has been offered in the intervening decades, most include the same underlying principles. Critical thinking refers to the use of cognitive skills or strategies that increase the probability of a desirable outcome. Critical thinking is purposeful, reasoned, and goal-directed. It is the kind of thinking involved in solving problems, formulating inferences, calculating likelihoods, and making decisions. Critical thinkers use these skills appropriately, without prompting, and usually with conscious intent, in a variety of settings. That is, they are predisposed to think critically. When we think critically, we are evaluating the outcomes of our thought processes—how good a decision is or how well a problem is solved (Halpern, 1996, 1998). This definition is broad enough to encompass a variety of viewpoints, so critical thinking can be taught as argument analysis (see, for example, Kahane, 1997), problem solving (Mayer, 1992), decision making (Dawes, 1988), or cognitive process (Rabinowitz, 1993). Regardless of the academic background of the instructor or the language used to describe critical thinking, all of these approaches share a set of common assumptions: there are identifiable critical thinking skills that can be taught and learned, and when students learn these skills and apply them appropriately, they become better thinkers.

Exciting Changes

For some college faculty, the new emphasis on critical thinking instruction has fundamentally altered what and how they teach. For example, there are several national efforts to teach statistics as a broadly applicable critical thinking skill, instead of teaching it as technique for data analysis (for example, Smith, 1995). Many of these new courses, with excellent materials for teaching and learning, are available on the Internet so that they can be adopted and modified by faculty who want to try new ways of teaching but do not know how to get started. A stellar example is a course called Chance, which has been designed to teach statistical principles using a variety of real-world problems and materials. It has an active Web site (www.dartmouth .edu /~chance/course/course.html) with courses being offered by local faculty on multiple college campuses, including Spelman, Grinnell, Dartmouth, Middlebury, and the University of Vermont. Real-life subject areas covered in these courses include polls and surveys, lotteries, AIDS, DNA fingerprinting, and smoking.

There are numerous places on the Web where faculty can find help if they want to change the focus of any course to make it more thinking skills based. Many of these sites are administered within individual disciplines. In psychology, the field I know best, there is a general-purpose site for college-level psychology courses called, appropriately, Psychplace. It contains learning activities designed to help students think critically about issues in the discipline (www.psychplace.com). One recent example from this site provides instruction in the use of argument analysis skills, featuring a debate by two psychologists over the importance of parents to the development of their children. In this example, critical thinking skills are applied to course content, with explicit instruction in both the skills and the content. Other teaching materials, including sample syllabi, reading lists, demonstrations, and learning activities, are collected at a site run by the division of the American Psychological Association dedicated to the teaching of psychology. The on-line materials are available, free of charge, at the Office of On-Line Teaching Resources in Psychology (www.lemoyne.edu/OTRP/).

The changing nature of technology has not only provided us with more and better ways to teach in general but has also increased the need for the skills of critical thinking. The easy availability, with just a few keystrokes, of massive amounts of information has made the ability to evaluate and sort information more important than ever. Furthermore, much of the information available on the Internet is not reliable, and some of it is deliberately and dangerously deceptive (as on sites that tout miracle cures for serious illnesses or offer deliberately biased accounts of history or current events). Thus the ability to judge the credibility of an information source has become an indispensable critical thinking skill that needs to be deliberately and repeatedly taught in college and earlier.

Dispositions for Critical Thinking

Another major change since the earlier editions of *New Directions for Teaching and Learning* that focused on critical thinking is the recognition that critical thinking instruction must also address student dispositions. It is not enough to teach college students the skills of critical thinking if they are not inclined to use them. Critical thinking is more than the successful use of the right skill in an appropriate context. It is also an attitude or disposition to recognize when a skill is needed and the willingness to exert the mental effort needed to apply it. Sears and Parsons (1991) call these dispositions the *ethic* of a critical thinker. Lazy or sloppy thinkers may have a large repertoire of critical thinking skills but not be inclined to use any of them. No one can develop expertise in any area without engaging in the effortful processes of thinking (see Wagner, 1997). Thus we need to find ways to make students value good thinking and the work that is needed to achieve that goal.

The How of Critical Thinking Instruction: A Four-Part Model

I recently proposed a four-part model of instruction for critical thinking (Halpern, 1998). Not surprisingly, it includes two parts we have already discussed—instruction in the skills and dispositions for critical thinking—but it also includes *structure training* as a means of improving the probability that students will recognize when a particular thinking skill is needed, even in a novel context. The problem in learning thinking skills that are needed in multiple contexts is that there are no obvious cues in the novel contexts that can trigger the recall of the thinking skill. With structure training, students are taught to create retrieval cues from the structural aspects of a problem or an argument so that when these structural aspects are present in the novel context, they can serve as cues for retrieval. I borrowed the term from Hummel and Holyoak (1997), who identified structure sensitivity as a fundamental property that underlies human thought: "First thinking is structure sensitive. Reasoning, problem solving, and learning . . . depend on a capacity to code and manipulate relational knowledge" (p. 427). For example, students may be able to explain why correlation is not causation when presented with this question on an exam but still not recognize that this same principle is operating when they read that children who attend religious schools score higher on standardized tests than those who attend public schools. Specific instruction in recognizing the structure of correlational problems can improve the probability that students will recognize these problems, even when the topic is different.

The last component of critical thinking instruction is *metacognitive monitoring*. *Metacognition* is usually defined as "what we know about what we know," so metacognitive monitoring is determining how we can use this knowledge to direct and improve the thinking and learning process. While engaging in critical thinking, students need to monitor their thinking process, checking that progress is being made toward an appropriate goal, ensuring accuracy, and making decisions about the use of time and mental effort. In the jargon of cognitive psychology, metacognitive monitoring serves the executive function of directing the thinking process. It is made overt and conscious during instruction, often by having instructors model their own thinking process, so that the usually private activity of thinking is made visible and open to scrutiny.

Using the Principles of Cognitive Psychology

Advances in critical thinking instruction have for the most part been based on the general principles of cognitive psychology, such as those discussed by Marilla Svinicki in Chapter One. Critical thinking instruction uses what we know about the way adults usually think and what has been effective in making positive changes to "thinking in the default mode." Some of the changes have resulted from changes in the world around us—for example, the new demands and challenges of technology; others have been based on past successes that have shown that it is possible to help college students think better. Although it is always tricky to predict the future, I believe that critical thinking instruction will continue to be an important component in college curricula. Workplace demands are becoming increasingly complex, and higher education is more important than ever before. As long as critical thinking is a desired outcome of education, we will need to find ways to help students improve their abilities to think critically and their disposition to use these skills.

References

Dawes, R. M. *Rational Choice in an Uncertain World.* Orlando, Fla.: Harcourt Brace, 1988.

Glaser, R. "Education and Thinking: The Role of Knowledge." *American Psychologist,* 1984, *39,* 93–104.

Halpern, D. F. *Thought and Knowledge: An Introduction to Critical Thinking.* (3rd ed.) Mahwah, N.J.: Erlbaum, 1996.

Halpern, D. F. "Teaching Critical Thinking for Transfer Across Domains: Disposition, Skills, Structure Training, and Metacognitive Monitoring." *American Psychologist,* 1998, *53,* 449–455.

Hummel, J. E., and Holyoak, K. J. "Distributed Representations of Structure: A Theory of Analogical Access and Mapping." *Psychological Review,* 1997, *104,* 427–466.

Kahane, H. *Logic and Contemporary Rhetoric.* (8th ed.) Belmont, Calif.: Wadsworth, 1997.

Lochhead, J., and Whimby, A. "Teaching Analytic Reasoning Through Think-Aloud Pair Problem Solving." In J. E. Stice (ed.), *Developing Critical Thinking and Problem-Solving Abilities.* New Directions for Teaching and Learning, no. 30. San Francisco: Jossey-Bass, 1987.

Mayer, R. E. *Thinking, Problem Solving, Cognition.* New York: Freeman, 1992.

National Education Goals Panel. *The National Education Goals Report: Building a Nation of Learners.* Washington, D.C.: U.S. Government Publishing Office, 1991.

Rabinowitz, M. (ed.). *Cognitive Science Foundations of Instruction.* Hillsdale, N.J.: Erlbaum, 1993.

Rubinstein, M. F., and Firstenberg, I. R. "Tools for Thinking." In J. E. Stice (ed.), *Developing Critical Thinking and Problem-Solving Abilities.* New Directions for Teaching and Learning, no. 30. San Francisco: Jossey-Bass, 1987.

Sears, A., and Parsons, J. "Toward Critical Thinking as an Ethic." *Theory and Research in Social Education,* 1991, *19,* 45–46.

Smith, P. C. "Assessing Writing and Statistical Competence in Probability and Statistics." *Teaching of Psychology,* 1995, *22,* 49–51.

Stice, J. E. *Developing Critical Thinking and Problem-Solving Abilities.* New Directions for Teaching and Learning, no. 30. San Francisco: Jossey-Bass, 1987.

Wagner, R. K. "Intelligence, Training, and Employment." *American Psychologist,* 1997, *52,* 1059–1069.

Woods, D. R. "How Might I Teach Problem Solving?" In J. E. Stice (ed.), *Developing Critical Thinking and Problem-Solving Abilities.* New Directions for Teaching and Learning, no. 30. San Francisco: Jossey-Bass, 1987.

Young, R. E. (ed.). *Fostering Critical Thinking.* New Directions for Teaching and Learning, no. 3. San Francisco: Jossey-Bass, 1980.

DIANE F. HALPERN is professor of psychology at California State University, San Bernardino.

6

The Seven Principles for Good Practice in Undergraduate Education were a huge success when they were first issued in the mid-1980s, and they have continued to be refined and used in a variety of ways since then.

Development and Adaptations of the Seven Principles for Good Practice in Undergraduate Education

Arthur W. Chickering, Zelda F. Gamson

Concern for improving undergraduate education has been unrelenting in the second half of the twentieth century. The two of us have been involved in many of these efforts and in the mid-1980s found ourselves in a position to pull together many of them under the rubric of Seven Principles for Good Practice in Undergraduate Education.

Origins of the Seven Principles for Good Practice

As one of the authors of "Involvement in Learning" (National Institute of Education, 1984), Gamson feared that this report and others that appeared within about a year of each other would not reach the faculty, administrators, and students to whom they were targeted (Bennett, 1984; Association of American Colleges and Universities, 1985; Newman, 1985). We both were members of the board of the American Association for Higher Education (AAHE), a broad-based national organization, and urged that it devote several of its national conferences to the improvement of undergraduate education. We also suggested that AAHE sponsor the development of a statement of the principles of a good undergraduate education.

Around the same time, we attended a conference at Wingspread, the conference center in Racine, Wisconsin, operated by the Johnson Foundation, which brought together the authors of several of the recent reports on undergraduate education along with other observers of higher education.

At this meeting, it became clear to us that the dissemination of a statement of principles could be timed to an undergraduate education reform movement that appeared to be sweeping the country.

All of the elements for this project were in place—two credible sponsoring organizations (AAHE and the Johnson Foundation), general discussion of the issues involved, and a broad-based national movement to improve undergraduate education. Drawing on the "principles of good practice in experiential learning" adapted from consumer groups by the Council on Adult and Experiential Learning (CAEL), an organization on whose founding board Chickering served and whose early history Gamson chronicled (Gamson, 1989), we decided to come up with a similar set of principles for undergraduate education.

How were we to generate such a statement? We wanted the statement to reflect the collective wisdom of the individuals who were most knowledgeable about the research literature. With support from the Johnson Foundation and the Lilly Endowment, we invited a small task force to meet for two days at Wingspread in the summer of 1986. The task force members included scholars who had conducted much of the research on the impact of the college experience as well as scholars of organizational, economic, and policy issues in higher education. The gathering was an extraordinary event in its own right. Though most of the participants knew one another's work, they had never come together to trace their work's implications for improving undergraduate education. We presented them with a number of principles we had drawn up ahead of time, with the caveat that they were to end up with no more than nine, preferably fewer.

We insisted that whatever we produced be accessible, understandable, practical, and widely applicable. Although everyone agreed that faculty were the primary audience, several task force members also felt that we should try to reach campus administrators, state higher education agencies, and government policymakers. The desire to reach multiple audiences reinforced the need to make the principles understandable and practical.

Development and Dissemination

The final version of the Seven Principles for Good Practice in Undergraduate Education was presented in the lead article in the March 1987 issue of the *AAHE Bulletin* (Chickering and Gamson, 1987). It said that good practice in undergraduate education

- Encourages student-faculty contact
- Encourages cooperation among students
- Encourages active learning
- Gives prompt feedback
- Emphasizes time on task
- Communicates high expectations
- Respects diverse talents and ways of learning

The response to the article was immediate and overwhelming, and it was soon republished as a special section in the June 1987 issue of the *Wingspread Journal*. More than 150,000 copies of the seven principles were ordered from the Johnson Foundation, and an untold number were copied or reprinted in other publications, such as newsletters of national associations and campus centers for teaching and learning.

We felt encouraged enough by the enthusiastic response to the statement of the principles to develop a self-assessment instrument for faculty members, with examples and indicators of each of the principles. We also decided to produce a second instrument with indicators of campus practices and policies in support of the seven principles. After much testing and circulating of ideas, inventories of good practice were published in 1989 by the Johnson Foundation in two handy self-assessment booklets (Chickering, Gamson, and Barsi, 1989).

The response to the inventories was again overwhelming. Within a week of publication, forty thousand were gone. After several printings, their distribution was taken over by Winona State University, which had established the Seven Principles Resource Center. Accounts of the seven principles and their adaptations and uses have appeared regularly since (Gamson and Poulsen, 1989; Heller, 1989; Chickering and Gamson, 1991; Hatfield, 1995). A veritable industry of commentary, research, and adaptation has followed.

Adaptations

We are aware of only some of the adaptations of the seven principles and do not intend to be exhaustive in those we present here, although they do illustrate the variety of follow-up activities and works in progress. The principles and the inventories have been incorporated in, adapted in, or used as the springboard for several similar assessment and research instruments. The earliest is the Student Inventory, available from the Seven Principles Resource Center at Winona State, which asks students to rate themselves according to indicators of each of the principles. Another student-oriented adaptation is the Seven Principles for Good Practice in Student Affairs, a collaborative effort of the American College Personnel Association and the National Association of Student Personnel Administrators.

The College Student Experiences Questionnaire is a well-developed research tool containing indicators that can be adapted to measure several of the seven principles. A new edition now includes some items that address more of the principles. This questionnaire has been used in several studies (Kuh and Vesper, 1997; Kuh, Pace, and Vesper, 1997).

Richard Webster at the Fisher College of Business, Ohio State University, has created the Learning Process Inventory and Assessment (LPIA), a survey-guided assessment based on the seven principles and the faculty, institutional, and student inventories. According to Webster, "The LPIA is a tool for helping faculty members communicate their subject matter to their students (that is, teaching content and teaching processes) and for helping students take more responsibility for . . . learning course content and managing their own learning process in more effective ways. This transfer of responsibility from teacher, instructor, or trainer to learner is one key to learning communities, in K–12, in higher education, and on the job" (personal communication, 1998).

Peter Ewell and his associates at the National Center for Higher Education Management Systems (NCHEMS) have incorporated the seven principles into a larger list of good practices (Ewell and Jones, 1996). These adaptations have appeared in an influential report issued by the Education Commission of the States, *Making Quality Count in Undergraduate Education* (1995). The report refers to twelve attributes of quality in undergraduate education:

- The organizational culture must have (1) high expectations, (2) respect for diverse talents and learning styles, and (3) an emphasis on the early years of study.
- A quality curriculum requires (4) coherence in learning, (5) synthesis of experiences, (6) ongoing practice of learned skills, and (7) integration of education and experience.
- Quality instruction incorporates (8) active learning, (9) assessment and prompt feedback, (10) collaboration, (11) adequate time on task, and (12) out-of-class contact with faculty.

Building on this work, Ewell led the creation of a survey of student engagement (National Survey of Student Engagement, n.d.), intended to provide information about the extent to which colleges and universities exhibit characteristics and commitments to high-quality undergraduate student outcomes. The results of the survey will be used to help colleges and universities improve the quality of their performance and offer data for making informed judgments to external assessors such as accrediting bodies and government agencies, as well as parents, students, and the media.

Applications

A variety of applications by institutions and individuals complement these adaptations of the principles and inventories. Perhaps the most systematic and extensive is described by Chuck Worth, director of institutional research at California State University, Chico. Worth reports:

> The seven principles have been broadly distributed and widely used. . . . This has been part of our overall university effort in strategic planning. The heart of our academic mission and the first goal of our strategic plan is student-centered learning. . . . It has been given to deans with encouragement to discuss [it] . . . with chairs and faculty. It has also been distributed and discussed at university leaders' strategic planning retreats, consisting of chairs, deans, academic senators, and key faculty. . . . Our president and provost gave two

$5,000 awards in a first annual recognition of an Outstanding Commitment to the Development of Student-Centered Learning Environments. A memo to all faculty and staff specifically mentioned the seven principles as a guide and partial criteria for the awards [personal communication, 1998].

The university has also used the seven principles in orientations for new faculty, in instruments for student assessment of the learning environment, and in student focus groups.

The seven principles have guided inquiry into the educational consequences of new communication and information technologies. At George Mason University, for example, a faculty technology survey asked whether computer technology encourages contact between faculty and students, encourages cooperation among students, and so on through the list of principles. The Flashlight Project, which uses the seven principles along with other ways of evaluating the impact of technology on student learning, offers opportunities for faculty to engage in discussions about technology (Chickering and Ehrmann, 1996). Karen Gentemann in the Office of Institutional Assessment at George Mason writes that in using the Flashlight Project materials, she has "been encouraging faculty to read some of the articles in which the principles are discussed" (personal communication, 1998).

The seven principles have also been deployed in professional development workshops. Peter Frederick, a professor of history at Wabash College, describes how he uses them: "I have used the seven principles as a standard first page for probably well over a hundred workshops I have done in the past decade throughout the nation. . . . The workshops are variously titled: 'Active Learning in the Classroom,' 'Revitalizing Traditional Forms of Teaching and Learning,' 'Empowering Learners for a Diverse Democratic Society.' The workshops are almost always interactive, [a format that allows me to] model the principles. . . . What prompted me to use them? They are pithy and make sound pedagogical sense. Pithiness is important for faculty, who do not want much educational theory" (personal communication, 1998). George Kuh, professor of higher education at Indiana University, who has used the seven principles "at least fifty times in presentations over the past few years," comments that "people always copy them down from the overhead and want copies" (personal communication, 1998).

Finally, we know about some of the individual faculty members who have applied the principles (Chickering and Gamson, 1991; Hatfield, 1995). An example is Jane Fraser, a professor of industrial and systems engineering at Ohio State University, who reports:

I have always tried to discuss my teaching methods with students. . . . I used the seven principles for a discussion of my teaching methods this quarter. I handed out the list to the class and also had the list on an overhead. I went through each principle, discussing how I am trying to accomplish it. I then discussed how each principle can be turned into a point of good learning—actions a student should take, not just actions the professor should take. . . .

Finally, I opened the discussion . . . about what principles they would add to the list. [The students] had some very good suggestions, especially along the lines that good practice involves conveying enthusiasm and presenting material in interesting ways [personal communication, 1998].

Research

The seven principles have inspired several lines of research. John Braxton and his colleagues looked at the tendency of different academic disciplines to enact the seven principles (Braxton, Olsen, and Simmons, 1998). They found that disciplines with "low paradigmatic development," such as history, psychology, and sociology—fields in which faculty are not in much agreement about the theory methods, techniques, and problems that are characteristics of the discipline—use four of the seven principles in their teaching: encouragement of student-faculty contact, encouragement of active learning, communication of high expectations, and respect for diverse talents and ways of knowing. George Kuh and his colleagues report on two studies based on the seven principles using the College Student Experiences Questionnaire. In a study of students' experiences at baccalaureate institutions and at doctoral degree granting universities, Kuh and Vesper (1997) found that students at the former reflected a positive effect of the seven principles, especially through increased faculty-student interaction between 1990 and 1994, and that students at the universities did not. In another study, Kuh, Pace, and Vesper (1997) found that faculty-student contact, cooperation among students, and active learning were the best predictors of student educational gains in college.

We are pleased that the seven principles have inspired such research and encourage others to make use of both the principles and the inventories in carrying out studies of teaching practices, student learning, faculty, disciplines, and institutions. Our greatest impact, however, is on individual faculty members and on institutions. As George Kuh pointed out to us, "There are many of your apostles out there who are translating and interpreting the principles as policies and practices are evaluated and developed. . . . You can see the images of these principles reflected in many of the initiatives we have under way on my campus and elsewhere. So [even if] folks may not be wearing a laminated SEVEN PRINCIPLES card around their necks, the principles have and will continue to have a substantial impact" (personal communication, 1998).

References

Association of American Colleges and Universities. *Integrity in the College Curriculum: A Report to the Academic Community*. Washington, D.C.: Association of American Colleges and Universities, 1985.
Bennett, W. J. *To Reclaim a Legacy: A Report on the Humanities in Higher Education*. Washington, D.C.: National Endowment for the Humanities, 1984.

Braxton, J. M., Olsen, D., and Simmons, A. "Affinity Disciplines and the Use of Principles of Good Practice for Undergraduate Education." *Research in Higher Education,* 1998, *39*(3), 299–318.

Chickering, A. W., and Ehrmann, S. C. "Implementing the Seven Principles: Technology as a Lever." *AAHE Bulletin,* 1996, *49*(2), 3–6.

Chickering, A. W., and Gamson, Z. F. "Seven Principles for Good Practice in Undergraduate Education." *AAHE Bulletin,* 1987, *39*(7), 3–7.

Chickering, A. W., and Gamson, Z. F. (eds.). *Applying the Seven Principles for Good Practice in Undergraduate Education.* New Directions for Teaching and Learning, no. 47. San Francisco: Jossey-Bass, 1991.

Chickering, A. W., Gamson, Z. F., and Barsi, L. *Inventories of Good Practice.* Milwaukee, Wis.: Johnson Foundation, 1989.

Education Commission of the States. *Making Quality Count in Undergraduate Education.* Denver, Colo.: Education Commission of the States, 1995.

Ewell, P., and Jones, D. *Indicators of "Good Practice" in Undergraduate Education: A Handbook for Development and Implementation.* Boulder, Colo.: National Center for Higher Education Management Systems, 1996.

Gamson, Z. F. *Higher Education and the Real World: The Story of CAEL.* Wolfeboro, N.H.: Longwood Academic, 1989.

Gamson, Z. F., and Poulsen, S. J. "Inventories of Good Practice: The Next Step for the Seven Principles for Good Practice in Undergraduate Education." *AAHE Bulletin,* 1989, *47*(3), 708–714.

Hatfield, S. R. (ed.). *The Seven Principles in Action: Improving Undergraduate Education.* Bolton, Mass.: Anker, 1995.

Heller, S. "Delighted Authors Find Their Agenda for Education Is a Huge Hit." *Chronicle of Higher Education,* Dec. 13, 1989, pp. A41, A43.

Kuh, G. D., and Vesper, N. "A Comparison of Student Experiences with Good Practices in Undergraduate Education Between 1990 and 1994." *Review of Higher Education,* 1997, *21*(1), 43–61.

Kuh, G. D., Pace, C., and Vesper, N. "The Development of Process Indicators to Estimate Student Gains Associated with Good Practices in Undergraduate Education." *Research in Higher Education,* 1997, *38*(4), 435–454.

National Institute of Education. *Involvement in Learning: Realizing the Potential of American Higher Education.* Washington, D.C.: U.S. Department of Education, 1984.

National Survey of Student Engagement. *The College Student Report.* Bloomington: National Survey of Student Engagement, Indiana University, n.d.

Newman, F. *Higher Education and the American Resurgence.* Princeton, N.J.: Carnegie Foundation for the Advancement of Teaching, 1985.

ARTHUR W. CHICKERING is visiting distinguished professor at Vermont College, Norwich University, Montpelier, Vermont; senior associate in the New England Resource Center of Higher Education; and visiting professor of higher education at the University of Massachusetts, Boston.

ZELDA F. GAMSON is senior associate and founding director of the New England Resource Center for Higher Education and professor emeritus at the University of Massachusetts, Boston.

7

Issues of diversity and inclusion have posed some serious challenges for higher education in the past and continue to do so today.

Taking Diversity Seriously: New Developments in Teaching for Diversity

Laura L. B. Border

New Directions volume 49, *Teaching for Diversity* (Border and Chism, 1992), discussed diverse learning styles, the implementation of universitywide diversity programs, feminist pedagogy, strategies for unbiased teaching, resources, and faculty and teaching assistant development programs in selected universities. At the time, few postsecondary institutions were effectively grappling with the diversification of the faculty, student body, curriculum, or teaching methods. Nancy Chism and I felt obliged to present moral, demographic, civic, and political arguments to convince instructors and institutions that they needed to attend to issues of diversity.

Today many of the campuses discussed in that volume have established programs, published materials, and revised their curricula. National conferences on diversity sponsored by the American Council of Education have emphasized the need to educate "all of one nation," and conferences of the American Association for Higher Education have focused on "difficult dialogues." Many institutions have diversity plans that involve all academic and support units. Student conferences such as the Big Twelve Conference on Student Employment Issues have addressed hiring constraints that still exist. Extensive collaborative efforts are in place that would have been unimaginable in the past, most notably the American Association of Colleges and Universities' Diversity Web.

Thus, despite backsliding in the political arena and continuing residential racial segregation in the United States, researchers and practitioners in postsecondary institutions have moved toward conscious and considered support for diversity efforts on their campuses. They also seem to be getting a grip on what works and what doesn't work. Faculty and administrators are attempting to actualize policies and programs to ensure that their graduates are educated citizens who have the ability, knowledge, and resolution to ensure democratic freedoms and responsibilities. A review of the current literature on diversity suggests that development has occurred in numerous areas, including terminology and focus, breadth and depth of activities, implementation of policies, and available resources.

Terminology and Focus

In 1992, common terminology was either legalistic or general—*affirmative action, pluralism, multiculturalism*—witnessing to the fact that no one wanted to assume individual responsibility for changing the existing state of affairs. As coeditors of the 1992 issue, Nancy Chism and I struggled to use terms that were appropriate, nonjudgmental, and yes, inoffensive, making the discussion obtuse and diffuse. The attempt to be inclusive is evident in the text where "minority male and women of all colors" seemed the only way to state the issue of discrimination and the term "white privilege" seemed too political and inflammatory to use in an argument being made to a predominantly white male academy. Affirmative action, racism, prejudice, and bias had just been defined by a seminal article in *Change* magazine, helping readers clarify their own positions in the discussion. The concept of *political correctness* had not yet appeared on the scene and in fact arose in reaction against the other terms. Religious prejudice was not discussed at all in the context of the *New Directions for Teaching and Learning* series, nor were other currently significant areas such as disability and sexual orientation.

Today's terminology reflects developments in conceptual frameworks and broader knowledge and experience in academe and in the general public. Changes are evident in the common usage of terms such as *lifelong education, identity formation, racialization, whiteness, civic responsibility, democracy*, and *community*. On the East Coast, the argument is often framed in terms of class—"health care for the poor and middle class," "job training for the poor and middle class" (Harney, 1999). In the West and Southwest, the discussion has shifted from treatises on affirmative action, pluralism, and multiculturalism to a verbal and written discourse on democracy. This change has occurred partly because of political backsliding in California and Texas but also because as serious individuals study, learn about, and begin to take diversity seriously, a realization of what America is all about starts to take shape. An appreciation for the wealth of experiences shared by our diverse citizenry surfaces in freshly stimulated minds, along with shame in the face of the limits of current postsecondary education. As the contributors to *Higher Education and American Commitments (HEAC)* have eloquently expressed it, concerns of equality and liberty rise to the fore and the belief that "democracy . . . the ideal that all human beings have equal value, deserve equal respect, and should be given equal opportunity to fully participate in the life and direction of the society" seems possible in the academy (Association of American Colleges and Universities, 1995, p. 9).

John Dewey first used the term *lifelong education,* but in the context of the academy it takes on a slightly different meaning. We are used to referring to lifelong education in our departments of continuing education where the terms conjure up images of students returning to evening classes to bone up on the latest in technology or to expand their education beyond the limits of their bachelor's degree experience. In the context of the postsecondary community, however, lifelong education calls into question the typical self-congratulatory aspect of the terminal degree. Doctorate-holding individuals often operate under the illusion that their education is complete and that they have nothing else to learn. The academy's experiences with diversity over the past three decades reduce this illusion to the figment of the imagination that it always was. Even those of us who have doctoral degrees still have new things to learn, and when it comes to dealing with diverse students and colleagues on our campuses, many of us have been ill prepared by our former education. Faculty and administrators need to avail themselves of the many opportunities that exist locally and nationally to enhance their skills and to learn more about the diverse world in which the university operates.

Identity Formation, Racialization, and Whiteness

The political power structure on U.S. campuses has long been aligned with concepts of racialization, which the authors of *HEAC* define as "that specific form of thinking by which human differences such as color come to be seen as socially significant and determinative" (Association of American Colleges and Universities, 1995, p. 25). The perceived whiteness of the American university led to the formation of the historically black colleges and universities in the late nineteenth century. One hundred years later, we are still struggling with educating people of all races on one campus. Native American scholars have recently begun to pursue the development of a university system that would meet the needs of their youth.

The concept of identity formation has become closely allied with diversity programs. Researchers and practitioners at the University of Massachusetts have contributed a formidable resource to academe in the form of their recent publication, *Teaching for Diversity and Social Justice: A Sourcebook* (Adams, Bell, and Griffin, 1997). Basing their work on that of Hardiman and Jackson (1992), they explain how identity development is directly related to one's position in a social, racial, or gendered structure and to social oppression of freedom within the group. One major aspect of this work is that it brings forth the concept of whiteness, allowing for a discussion of the impact of race in academic interactions and institutions and negating the historical perspective of "American identity as 'white,' the nega-tion of racial otherness" (Association of American Colleges and Universities, 1995, p. 27).

Civic Responsibility, Democracy, and Community

As campuses across the country have confronted the many issues that arise when formulating a diversity plan or revising the curriculum of a depart-ment or college, community dialogue begins to occur. As Maxine Greene has observed, the university, as an "authentic public space," is "a space of dialogue and possibility" (Association of American Colleges and Universities, 1995, p. 36). Institutions and organizations can believe in and foster change, but then comes the realization that change changes the institution and the organization. Two large national organizations have in the past year experi-enced major confrontations at national conferences regarding conflicting viewpoints on diversity issues. In each case, the incident resulted in changed programming for the national conferences and increased dialogue between constituencies. Conflict resolution theory teaches that a group is not a group until it learns to manage conflict effectively. Diversity is an issue that cuts across all aspects of an organization, personal, intellectual, social, and polit-ical. In the formation of community, groups have to learn to resolve differ-ences and identify common goals.

While organizations and campuses across the nation are struggling to define diversity statements, policies, and activities, the American Indian Science and Engineering Society (AISES) operates on the basis of its "value statements." These statements are well suited to the development of civic responsibility, democracy, and community on our college campuses and in our professional organization (see Exhibit 7.1).

Breadth and Depth of Activities

Today's university is being called on to balance the inequities of misplaced and misunderstood liberties and the excesses of the majority while making sure that minority groups are granted the benefits of the ideals on which this country was founded. Immediately following the passage of the Civil Rights Act in 1964, a flurry of activity occurred at the national level in the formation of associations to support this goal. For example, the American Association for Higher Education was founded in 1966 to create a forum in which administrators could meet to discuss pertinent issues. The Profes-sional and Organizational Development Network was formed in 1975 by faculty for faculty to help one another find more effective means of instruc-tion, especially in view of the changes occurring in student populations. The American Council of Education opened its Office of Minorities in Higher Education in 1987 and has published sixteen reports on the status of minorities since then. The Western Interstate Commission on Higher

Exhibit 7.1. Value Statements of the American Indian Science and Engineering Society

---

Trust. AISES will create a loving environment of trust through an open system that embraces integrity, self-confidence, confidentiality, and honesty.

Excellence. AISES is committed to excellence in carrying out the mission with a spirit of dedication and motivation.

Service. AISES will serve the community with a sense of generosity, caring, compassion, and a responsibility of giving back.

Integrity. Having the strength and will to do the right thing.

Honesty. Is the best Indian policy.

Spirituality. Respecting the beliefs and values of others.

Compassion. Walking in another person's moccasins—helping.

Mother Earth and fry bread. Making oneself available and offering of oneself.

Commitment. Is walking the talk and staying aligned with our vision.

Humor. Good humor is essential to lighten the tensions of the tasks.

Sobriety. AISES policy embodies sobriety to optimize the development of American Indian people.

Respect. A reflection in you of the community and your values.

Education (WICHE) also began publishing data from studies on diversity efforts while developing consultation efforts aimed at educating postsecondary administrators.

At the end of the 1980s, the academy was shaken by the publication of several diatribes lamenting the demise of the idealized concept of a liberal education grounded uniquely in the Greek and European traditions. These critiques were written by once complacent faculty who had suddenly realized that life in the American university had irrevocably changed. Alan Bloom and Dinesh D'Souza made frantic attempts to contain the roaring river of diversity, flooding the media and radio talk shows with politicized jargon and slogans like political correctness. The major national educational organizations responded by making diversity a priority in their programming for national conferences, in their sponsored research projects, and in their publications.

Over the past decade, graduate education has begun to shift as well. For example, efforts are being made to bring students from underrepresented groups into graduate school, the precursor to diversifying the faculty. Currently, WICHE is involved in the Compact for Faculty Diversity, a collaboration between universities and disciplinary organizations designed for just such a purpose.

Now, at the end of the millennium, the floodwaters of diversity are coursing through American higher education. This growth has resulted in an incredible array of programs, policies, campus diversity plans, and Web sites that bear witness to the vigor of diversity activities on campuses throughout America. *HEAC*'s definition—"Diversity refers to the variety created in any society (and within any individual) by the presence of different points of view and ways of making meaning which generally flow from the influence of different cultural and religious heritages, from the differences in how we socialize women and men, and from the differences that emerge from class, age, and developed ability" (Association of American Colleges and Universities, 1995, pp. 9–10)—only hints at the possible growth that can occur when such diverse perspectives converge in educational institutions.

A typical campus at the end of the century is likely to have a diversity statement published by the governing board and a campuswide diversity plan that is supported by the diversity plans of each individual unit. Links are being made between diversity and performance-based budgeting. As more and more campuses develop Web sites, more profile their diversity components. Campuses continue to add faculty and teaching assistant development programs that offer programming and consultation that integrate diversity into improved options for unbiased teaching methodology. Faculty affairs personnel have drawn up recruiting and hiring policies that support the selection of faculty from underrepresented groups according to departmental needs. Students on campuses find cultural centers provided for their support. Staff development centers offer workshops, consultation, and training in diversity and sexual harassment issues. Campuses that still have no resource center for women and nontraditional students will find that these things are now central to recruitment and retention. Multiple programs to support undergraduate students, women in traditionally white male fields, and students of every ethnic or linguistic group are viewed as essential to the campus mission. Curricular development broadens and deepens each discipline's content and method by bringing in aspects that go beyond the narrow European and American lens. Students are demanding that their campuses be more inclusive and diverse.

Expanded Activities to Support Diversity

Who needs to attend to issues of diversity? The faculty, the administration, the faculty developers (whose ranks have swollen noticeably since 1992), and last but not least, the graduate students who teach on our campuses. The Ford Foundation's survey of registered voters in the fall of 1998 (DYG, 1998) demonstrates the American public's commitment to diversity efforts. Nearly 70 percent of the more than two thousand respondents agreed that explicit steps should be taken to ensure diversity in the student and faculty populations and that diversity contributes positively to the general atmosphere of a campus and the education of its students. This strong public mandate should encourage all postsecondary institutions to increase the rate at which students from all groups matriculate in and graduate from their institutions.

College and university administrators are responsible not only for ensuring that all students reach their academic potential but also for ensuring their safety and social comfort in interactions in classrooms, residence halls, and elsewhere on campus. They also ensure that students have equal access to opportunities for employment, professional development, support services, and the pursuit of graduate and professional degrees. Our colleges and universities are perfect examples of what has been called the "contact zone . . . the space in which peoples geographically and historically separated come into contact with each other and establish ongoing relations" (Association of American Colleges and Universities, 1995, p. 32). They are also perfect places to practice what the authors of *HEAC* describe as a democratic manner, the "practices and dispositions—manners—toward others that enable them to discharge their duties as neighbors, within and across communities" (p. 32).

References

Adams, M., Bell, L. A., and Griffin, P. (eds.). *Teaching for Diversity and Social Justice: A Sourcebook.* New York: Routledge, 1997.

Association of American Colleges and Universities. "The Drama of Diversity and Democracy." In Association of American Colleges and Universities, *Higher Education and American Commitments.* Washington, D.C.: Association of American Colleges and Universities, 1995.

Border, L.L.B., and Chism, N. V. (eds.). *Teaching for Diversity.* New Directions for Teaching and Learning, no. 49. San Francisco: Jossey-Bass, 1992.

DYG, Inc. *Campus Diversity Initiative.* Dearborn, Mich.: Ford Foundation, 1998.

Hardiman, R., and Jackson, B. W. "Racial Identity Development: Understanding Racial Dynamics in College Classrooms and on Campus." In M. Adams (ed.), *Promoting Diversity in College Classrooms: Innovative Responses for the Curriculum, Faculty, and Institutions.* New Directions for Teaching and Learning, no. 52. San Francisco, Calif.: Jossey-Bass, 1992.

Harney, J. O. "The Future of New England." *Connection* (New England Board of Higher Education), Feb. 1999.

LAURA L. B. BORDER is director of the Graduate Teaching Assistant Program of the University of Colorado, Boulder.

*The past decade has seen dramatic growth in the use of
educational technology by college faculty, particularly
Internet applications and the delivery of courses via
distance education. Computer-based technologies have
opened doors to a vast array of new learning
opportunities because they are ideally suited for
a student-centered educational environment.*

Teaching in the Information Age:
A New Look

Michael J. Albright

Several years ago, David Graf and I edited *New Directions for Teaching and
Learning (NDTL)* volume 51, titled *Teaching in the Information Age: The Role
of Educational Technology* (Albright and Graf, 1992) to examine then-
current trends in instructional technology and to discuss their implications
for teaching and learning in the postsecondary setting. It was the first *NDTL*
volume dedicated entirely to educational technology since number 9, edited
by Christopher Knapper (1982) ten years earlier. Although the surge of
interest in technology and its pedagogical applications during the 1990s can
hardly be attributed to *NDTL* volume 51, it met an emerging need and was
one of the best-selling publications in the series.

A nationwide survey conducted in 1994 for the Corporation for Public Broadcasting (CPB) (Russell, Collier, and Hancock, 1995) found that faculty use of classroom technologies was more widespread than perhaps many
of us realized. More than half (54 percent) of the two thousand randomly
selected responding faculty reported that they had used video-based instructional materials during the fall 1993 academic term, and two-thirds said
they had used video for instructional purposes in the past. Twenty-nine percent had used a computer in the classroom to give a demonstration or presentation at least once during the fall 1993 term, and 42 percent said they
had done so in the past. Fifteen percent reporting using multimedia materials (defined in the survey as computer-mediated integration of text, audio,
or video) during a fall 1993 course.

Kenneth Green's annual campus computing surveys have documented
a steady growth in faculty use of Internet technologies in teaching and learning. Green (1998) found that 44 percent of the courses at participating

91

institutions used electronic mail for instructional purposes in 1998, compared with 33 percent in 1997 and 25 percent in 1996. Nearly a fourth (23 percent) maintained Web pages for course materials and resources, up from 8 percent in 1996. Survey respondents estimated that 52 percent of all faculty and 45 percent of the undergraduates on their campuses used the Internet on a daily basis in 1998.

These studies illustrate a transformation that is slowly but steadily affecting college teaching. The CPB survey confirmed that conventional classroom technologies are still in high demand among faculty. These media are used primarily in large group settings for purposes such as providing organizational structure and facilitating note-taking, visualizing course content, providing stimuli for class activities, and taking students where they otherwise could not go—for example, to Antarctica or into a blood cell or five hundred years into the past. They allow all students to share the same learning experiences and permit faculty members to integrate these technologies into their lectures and engage the entire class in discussion of the materials viewed.

A pervasive myth in higher education is that these conventional classroom media are dead and that computer-based technologies represent the wave of the future. Although the second part of that statement is undeniably true, the CPB survey clearly demonstrated the folly of the first part. Classroom media will not be dead until the lecture as a form of teaching is dead, an era we are not likely to encounter until long after most readers of this volume are cashing in their retirement pensions.

Computer-based technologies, however, have opened the doors to a vast array of new learning opportunities for students. These technologies are much more personal and individualized. They provide hands-on learning experiences. They are ideally suited for use in a learner-centered instructional environment because they so strongly promote active learning, collaboration, mastery of course material, and student control over the learning process. Digital learning technologies can perform many of the same functions as conventional classroom media, but other functions go well beyond the capabilities of videotapes and transparencies. For example, new technologies can do all of the following:

- Facilitate in-depth learning
- Promote inquiry, construction of knowledge, and development of insights
- Promote creativity and enable revision (multiple drafts) and improvement
- Provide greatly expanded access to information
- Enable students to obtain current, literally up-to-the-minute information
- Expand course discussions beyond the classroom and enable participation by experts and resource persons anywhere in the world
- Customize learning experiences to meet individual student needs and accommodate differing learning styles

- Promote real-world learning that better prepares students for the workplace
- Promote learning of scholarly research tools
- Facilitate course outreach to whole new populations of distant learners

Significant Developments of the 1990s

What are the most important developments in educational technology since publication of volume 51? I propose four nominees: the World Wide Web, electronic mail and mailing lists, distance education, and technology classrooms.

World Wide Web. Perhaps no single entity represents the evolution of technology over the past decade more pointedly than the World Wide Web (WWW). The chapters for volume 51 were written during the fall and winter of 1991–1992, and the term *World Wide Web* appears nowhere in the issue. Conceived by the European Center for Particle Research (CERN) in 1989 as a means for sharing information among scientists, the Web did not become a playground for the masses until Mosaic was released as a Web *browser* in September 1993. Even after the introduction of Netscape as the next generation Web browser in late 1994, growth of the Web was restrained until the Internet itself was turned over to private telecommunications carriers in 1995 and its full-scale commercialization began. No more than 25,000 Web sites existed worldwide in mid-1995, but by the end of 1998 the total had exceeded 3.5 million.

College faculty have found much to like in the World Wide Web as an instructional tool. First, it is a remarkable source of information for class assignments, although searching the Web can be a formidable challenge, and students must bring their critical thinking skills to bear in evaluating the credibility of what they find (see Chapter Five). A survey conducted by the NEC Research Institute at Princeton University in early 1998 identified more than 320 million Web pages (Kolata, 1998). Although many of these were student shrines to their favorite rock stars and others of a strictly personal or trivial nature, the Web holds a vast storehouse of valuable information easily available at the student's fingertips.

Second, the Web offers extensive possibilities for interpersonal communication. David Woolley (1998) maintains a Web site providing information about more than a hundred conferencing systems that participants access via Web browsers. Many faculty are now using software such as Allaire Forums, FirstClass, InTandem, and Caucus for both synchronous and asynchronous conferencing and collaboration, with course-related messages maintained apart from participants' regular e-mail.

Third, we are seeing explosive growth in the number of course Web sites maintained by faculty for their students, both as supplements to conventional lecture courses and as *virtual* courses, with no face-to-face meetings.

Since 1996, more than thirty Web course products that integrate content delivery, communication, testing, and management tools within easily customized templates accessible to both faculty members and students via Web browsers have entered the marketplace. This list includes widely used tools such as WebCT, CourseInfo, Web Course in a Box, Intrakal, and TopClass. As a measure of the intense interest these products have generated, consider that within fourteen months after its introduction in 1997, WebCT had been licensed by more than six hundred institutions in thirty-three countries (Goldberg, 1998).

Partnerships have evolved between Web course product vendors and textbook publishers in which publishers create Web-based course materials to supplement their most popular textbooks, built on the architecture of the Web course product. The materials are normally installed on campus servers, and adopting faculty members can customize them in any way desired. Students receive password access upon purchase of the textbook. By the end of 1998, WebCT's list of publisher collaborators included Prentice Hall, Harcourt Brace (including Dryden Press and Holt, Rinehart and Winston), John Wiley and Sons, W. W. Norton, and Addison Wesley Longman. TopClass had similar arrangements with McGraw-Hill and Macmillan. Epstein (1998) noted that the Web is significantly changing the publisher-professor relationship, with publishers assuming the role of course Web master, creating Web-based materials and learning activities to supplement the course text and providing current news and information to update the text via the Web.

Electronic Mail and Mailing Lists. Steve Gilbert, president of the TLT Group, the teaching, learning, and technology affiliate of the American Association for Higher Education (AAHE), observed that electronic mail has "become the single most important instructional application of information technology" (1997, p. 1). More than half the faculty in Green's campus computing survey (1998) used e-mail for course communications. Electronic mail is personal, individualized, and highly interactive, and it serves as a poster technology for student-centered teaching.

The listserv list management software has been used by faculty for course-related, asynchronous group discussions since the heyday of BitNet in the 1980s. Majordomo and ListProcessor listservers were introduced in the 1990s, and many campuses provide one of these three to their faculty for group communications. Mailing lists extend course discussions outside the classroom, permit on-line discussions with scholars and other resource persons from other locations, and allow students to collaborate with other classes, including those at other universities worldwide. In addition to course mailing lists, more than ninety thousand public mailing lists on every conceivable topic enable students to obtain current information, become involved in discussions of issues with professionals around the world, and make and maintain professional contacts that often result in long-term collaborations and friendships.

Distance Education. Distance education is academe's most prominent growth industry at the turn of the millennium. Levenburg and Major (1998) noted distance education's potential to "drastically change the teaching and learning paradigm" (p. 4) by extending student access to programs and courses and enabling colleges and universities to tap new markets without significant investments in bricks and mortar. "Anytime, anywhere" learning opportunities, provided through communications technologies, have become so pervasive during the past decade that some observers have declared distance to be irrelevant (Saba, 1999). A survey by the higher education research firm InterEd estimated that over one million U.S. college students were enrolled in distance education courses in 1997, with that number expected to triple by 2001 (Gubernick and Ebeling, 1997).

By mid-1998, more than eight hundred U.S. colleges and universities offered degree courses via the Internet. TeleEducation NB, a distance education network in New Brunswick, Canada, maintains a comprehensive database of on-line courses; by the end of February 1999, the database included more than 12,500 courses from twenty countries. TeleEducation director Rory McGeal ("TeleCampus," 1998) predicted that more than forty thousand on-line courses would be available by the year 2000. An entire industry has arisen, led by companies such as Real Education and Convene, to partner with colleges to put courses and degree programs on the Internet.

Interinstitutional collaborations have become common. Perhaps the most visible has been the Western Governors University (WGU), a degree-granting institution with affiliated universities from Indiana to Guam and a partnership with Britain's well-established Open University. Other consortia do not grant degrees but broker distance education courses offered by their member institutions. In early 1999, the Southern Regional Education Board (SREB) listed more than twelve hundred courses offered by 175 colleges and universities in sixteen southeastern states. At that time, the California Virtual University (CVU) brokered 1,950 courses from 111 member institutions, registering 27,300 students. The Community College Distance Learning Network (CCDLN), a consortium of some of the most prominent community colleges and districts active in distance education, was formed in 1998 to share courses and move into new markets. Statewide higher education distance learning consortia have also been established in Colorado, Michigan, and Kentucky, and some individual institutions have set up their own partnerships. For example, Franklin University in Ohio has formed collaborations with more than fifty community colleges, enabling associate degree graduates to remain at their local campuses and complete baccalaureate degrees in business administration, computer science, and health services administration via on-line courses from Franklin.

AAHE vice president Ted Marchese (1998) painted an eye-opening and in many respects chilling picture of how the postsecondary landscape is being reshaped by commercial and nonprofit competitors, national and regional collaborations, and college-industry partnerships. Marchese specifically pointed to the University of Phoenix, with forty-eight thousand degree-credit students at fifty-seven learning centers in twelve states, as of mid-1998, as "the surest conversation-stopper today" (p. 1) in American higher education.

Technology Classrooms. On campus, the classroom environment itself is changing. Most college classrooms were initially designed to accommodate the chalk-and-talk teaching paradigm. Despite the widespread absence of specific campus plans to build or retrofit technology-enhanced classroom facilities (Blackett and Stanfield, 1994), the development of *smart classrooms* (Niemeyer and Black, 1994), with permanently installed video or data projection systems, computers (or computer interfaces), document cameras, VCRs, network access, control panels, and conventional media technologies such as overhead and slide projectors, has been a consistent trend at many institutions throughout the 1990s.

The very concept of the classroom is slowly changing. Conway (1998) has described a variety of high-technology learning environments that emphasize student collaboration, project work, and the use of technology as learning tools. She noted that "tomorrow's classrooms will be part of an integrated human and technological system that enables students to learn in a more dynamic and participatory way" (p. 200).

Intellectual Property Issues

Intellectual property issues, particularly those related to the Internet and distance education, have become more prominent and much more complex during the past decade and have come under the intense scrutiny of faculty organizations such as the American Association of University Professors (AAUP) (Cate and others, 1998). These concerns appear in two major contexts. The first is faculty ownership when their course materials are transformed into CD-ROMs and other multimedia (Gorman, 1998) and Web courses (Guernsey and Young, 1998). The consensus solution is for faculty and administrators at each institution to develop and maintain clearly defined intellectual property policies and royalty allocation agreements.

The other context is the "fair use" of copyrighted materials by faculty and students in the teaching and learning context. The current U.S. copyright law, enacted in 1976, was designed by its authors to be flexible but has many shortcomings when applied to digital age technologies. The Clinton administration convened the Conference on Fair Use (CONFU) in 1994 to address fair use issues in the digital environment. Representatives of proprietary, educational, and government organizations met collectively and in work groups to develop fair use guidelines for distance learning, image collections, multimedia, electronic reserves, and interlibrary loan. Two-and-a-half years later, only the multimedia guidelines existed in a form that could be presented to Congress, and the CONFU effort essentially disintegrated. Even the multimedia guidelines were not widely embraced by the education and library communities.

The Future

In just a few years, this chapter will likely seem as outdated as *NDTL* volume 51 seems now. My predictions for the first decade of the new millennium include the following:

Next-generation Internet capabilities that greatly expand available bandwidth, enabling real-time, digital video-based communication and distribution of courses and resources around the world

A continuation of the explosive growth of distance education and, for institutions that do not engage in partnerships with other institutions or industry, significantly increased competition for students

Wider adoption of student-centered learning activities involving Internet and multimedia resources by faculty in teaching their on-campus courses

A gradual integration of digital versatile disk (DVD) into teaching and learning, via replacement of CD-ROM drives with DVD-ROM drives in computers and with DVD-video players in place of videocassette players

Continued evolution of the concept of the textbook as a customizable resource composed of traditional print, digital media (CD-ROM or DVD-ROM), and Web-based materials

More classrooms equipped with permanently installed technology equipment and fewer served by portable equipment

A worsening of what Steve Gilbert (1998) calls the "support service crisis," the lack of sufficient resources to enable academic technology support units to keep up with rapidly expanding faculty needs and expectations

Gradual replacement of faculty who refuse to incorporate technology into their teaching until they see some evidence that students learn better from technology than from chalk-and-talk lectures.

References

Albright, M. J., and Graf, D. L. (eds.). *Teaching in the Information Age: The Role of Educational Technology.* New Directions for Teaching and Learning, no. 51. San Francisco: Jossey-Bass, 1992.

Blackett, A., and Stanfield, B. "A Planner's Guide to Tomorrow's Classrooms." *Planning for Higher Education,* 1994, 22(3), 25–31.

Cate, F. H., Gumport, P., Hauser, R., Richardson, J., Wexman, V., Alger, J., and Smith, M. "Issues in Colleges and Universities." *Academe,* 1998, 84(3), 39–45.

Conway, K. L. "Designing Classrooms for the 21st Century." In D. G. Oblinger and S. C. Rush (eds.), *The Future-Compatible Campus: Planning, Designing, and Implementing Information Technology in the Academy.* Bolton, Mass.: Anker, 1998.

Epstein, S. L. "An Alternative to Faculty as Full-Time Web Master." *Syllabus,* 1998, 12(2), 56–57.

Gilbert, S. W. "Email, Communications, Seasons Greetings!" AAHESGIT [On-line]. Dec. 14, 1997. Available via e-mail: AAHESGIT@list.cren.net.

Gilbert, S. W. "Punished for Success." AAHESGIT [On-line]. Dec. 4, 1998. Available via e-mail: AAHESGIT@list.cren.net.

Goldberg, M. "How Widespread Is WebCT?" WebCT-Users [On-line]. Dec. 3, 1998. Available via e-mail: webct-users@webct.com.

Gorman, R. A. "Intellectual Property: The Rights of Faculty as Creators and Users." *Academe,* 1998, *84*(3), 14–18.

Green, K. C. *The 1998 National Survey of Information Technology in Higher Education.* Encino, Calif.: Campus Computing Project, 1998.

Gubernick, L., and Ebeling, A. "I Got My Degree Through E-Mail." *Forbes,* June 15, 1997, pp. 84–92.

Guernsey, L., and Young, J. R. "Who Owns On-Line Courses?" *Chronicle of Higher Education,* June 5, 1998, pp. A21–A23.

Knapper, C. K. (ed.). *Expanding Learning Through New Communications Technologies.* New Directions for Teaching and Learning, no. 9. San Francisco: Jossey-Bass, 1982.

Kolata, G. "It's Confirmed: Web's Size Bogs Down Searches." *New York Times,* Apr. 9, 1998, p. G3.

Levenburg, N. M., and Major, H. T. "Distance Learning: Implications for Higher Education in the 21st Century." *Technology Source,* Nov. 1998. [http://horizon.unc.edu/TS/commentary/1998-11.asp].

Marchese, T. "Not-So-Distant Competitors: How New Providers Are Remaking the Postsecondary Marketplace." *AAHE Bulletin,* May 1, 1998. [www.aahe.org/bulletin/bull_1may98.htm].

Niemeyer, D., and Black, B. "Smart Classrooms at the University of Colorado at Boulder." Paper presented at the Annual Convention of the Association for Educational Communications and Technology, Nashville, Feb. 18, 1994.

Russell, S. H., Collier, M. H., and Hancock, M. P. *1994 Study of Communications Technology in Higher Education: Final Report.* Menlo Park, Calif.: SRI International, 1995. (ED 404 931)

Saba, F. "The Death of Distance and the Rise of the Network Society." *Distance Education Report,* 1999, *3*(1), 1–2.

"TeleCampus International Online Course Database." *Distance Education Report,* 1998, *2*(12), 7.

Woolley, D. R. "Conferencing Software for the Web." Oct. 24, 1998. [http://thinkofit.com/webconf/].

MICHAEL J. ALBRIGHT is associate director of New Media Services, California State University, Monterey Bay.

PART THREE

And Now What?

9

What does the future hold for New Directions for
Teaching and Learning?

New Directions for *New Directions?*

Marilla D. Svinicki

These days, educators seem to be polishing up their crystal balls and shuf-
fling their Tarot cards to make predictions about what the next century will
bring. It seems only fitting that I should do so, too, although perhaps it
would be more appropriate to adopt a more research-based approach for this
issue. Therefore, in this chapter, I will look ahead a bit to see what new ideas
for *New Directions* might come out of projected changes in higher education
and its study.

Future Forces

I had the great good fortune recently of being asked to present a paper titled
"Teachers for the Twenty-First Century" at the Improving University Learning and Teaching annual conference in Australia. My reading in the literature in preparation for that presentation about what might be coming down
the road convinced me to focus on five forces that seem to have some
important implications for teaching (Svinicki, 1999):

- The spread of technology
- The commercialization of higher education
- Increased cross-disciplinary emphasis
- Internationalization of fields and students
- Increasing pressure to serve the community

During the discussion that followed, participants in the session brain-
stormed how each of these potential forces might affect four areas of teaching expertise: content knowledge, pedagogical knowledge, interpersonal
skills, and orientation toward teaching. (For an example of how the matrix

crossing these two dimensions of forces and teaching expertise works, visit the Web site at www.utexas.edu/academic/cte/teach/IUT.html.) It was a really interesting discussion, as we identified areas where current teachers might have to build new expertise to cope with the coming changes in higher education. For example, looking at how technology intersects with interpersonal skills, instructors will have to learn to develop those important teacher-student relationships on-line as the use of electronic communication increases.

In thinking about that session and the future of *New Directions,* I can see how looking forward in that way could suggest issue topics that will be coming in the future. In fact, there is an issue in development right now that addresses the very topic of interpersonal skills I just used as an example. In addition to the forces cited, *New Directions* will probably deal with issues concerning the following trends in higher education:

New pedagogical skills. New instructional methods are being developed on a regular basis. With each new method come new skills that instructors need.

New students. Our student body is diversifying in many different ways. With the advent of greater access due to technology, this can only increase. We need to keep up with the characteristics of these new students and the best ways to facilitate their learning.

New structures. Higher education institutions are changing administratively and departmentally in response to changes in field emphasis and to outside competition. New structures bring with them new responsibilities for teachers and students alike.

New teachers. The very nature of the faculty is changing. The increases in nontraditional faculty parallel the changes in students and the changes in structures. These fresh perspectives offer interesting challenges to traditional thoughts about teaching and learning.

Of course, it is probable that future issues will also delve into areas we haven't even thought of yet.

Preparing to Meet the Challenge

With so many potential changes facing the faculty of tomorrow, how will the field of teaching in higher education itself change? I see three very hopeful signs that we are developing in directions that will allow us to cope.

A new respect for the complexity of teaching and learning. The first hopeful sign is that the old adage of "all you need to know to teach is your content" is losing steam. At my own institution and in the broader content of higher education in general, I see signs that faculty from fields outside education are beginning to acknowledge that there may be more to teaching than telling. The existence of "pedagogical content knowledge" is starting to be accepted. If the trend continues, educational research and theory may have a chance of becoming respectable as a focus of study. That would certainly be a boost for publications like *New Directions,* which tries to bring the complexities of research and theory to the faculty.

The desire for a theoretical foundation for teaching. I also see a trend in faculty interest that goes beyond the "bag of teaching tricks" characterization that has plagued faculty development since the beginning. I cannot say that faculty have altogether abandoned their demands for guidance on what to do in class on Monday morning, but they do seem to be more open to the idea that there might be good theoretical reasons for doing whatever they're planning for Monday. Because a strong component of *New Directions* has been to make the connection between theory and practice, this interest in knowing why as well as what fits us quite well.

A renewed interest in classroom research. With the influential classroom research movement has come an interest in asking and answering questions about one's own class. To me, this is the perfect melding of the theoretical ("Why does my class do that?") and the practical ("What can I do about it?"). It is the stuff of future *New Directions* issues in which we can blend these two areas of interest and from it fashion a stronger base for teaching and learning.

The Role of *New Directions*

I believe that *New Directions'* long history of serving as a meeting place of theory, research, and practice will be even more important in the coming years because of the forces and trends in play. The series has always tried to be the first source for information about teaching, and we will continue to emphasize the pragmatics of teaching. But I think we can challenge faculty of the future to look beyond the immediate and start building a strong foundation for teaching and learning in higher education. As evidenced by the chapters in Part One of this issue, much good work is already available to inform practice. Helping faculty become aware of what has gone before and encouraging them to use it and go beyond it will be the continuing challenge for this series in the next century.

Reference

Svinicki, M. D. "Teachers for the Twenty-First Century: From Gatekeepers to Guide-posts." Paper presented at the International Improving University Learning and Teaching Conference, Griffith University, Brisbane, Australia, July 6, 1999.

MARILLA D. SVINICKI is editor-in-chief of the New Directions for Teaching and Learning *series and is director of the Center for Teaching Effectiveness and senior lecturer in the Department of Educational Psychology at the University of Texas at Austin.*

INDEX

Abercrombie, M.L.J., 57
Abrami, P. C., 41
Active learning, 34, 57, 76
Adams, M., 18, 85
Affirmative action, 84
Albright, M. J., 91
Aleamoni, L. M., 42
Alexander, P., 9, 17
Alger, J., 96
American Association of Colleges and Universities, Diversity Web, 83
American Association for Higher Education (AAHE): on diversity, 83; formation of, 86; group-based pedagogies promoted by, 57; Seven Principals for Good Practice and, 75, 76
American Association of University Professors (AAUP), 96
American College Personnel Association, 77
American Council of Education, 83; Office of Minorities in Higher Education, 86
American Indian Science and Engineering Society (AISES), 86, 87
Ames, C., 21, 22
Ames, R., 22
Aminzade, R., 46, 47
Andersen, J. F., 63
Andersen, P. A., 63
Anderson, J. A., 18
Anderson, J. R., 8
Anderson, R. C., 16
Angelo, T. A., 10, 39
Arendale, D. R., 13
Arreola, R. A., 42
Assessment: of teaching, 39–42; of use of good practices, 77. See also Evaluation
Association of American Colleges and Universities, diversity and, 75, 85, 86, 88, 89
Atkinson, J. W., 20
Attribution theory, 21
Ausubel, D. P., 9

Bakker, P. A., 10
Bandura, A., 20
Banner, J. M., 62

Barsi, L., 77
Baxter-Magolda, M. B., 18
Beaudry, J., 18
Behavior theory, 5–8; instructional implications of, 6–8; on motivation, 19–20
Behavioral objectives, 6, 7
Beidler, P. G., 62
Bekey, J., 39
Bell, L. A., 85
Bennett, W. J., 75
Bereiter, C., 13
Bethany, B. H., 33
Birch, D., 20
Black, B., 96
Blackett, A., 96
Bloom, A., 87
Bloom, B. S., 6, 30
Boice, R., 45
Bomotti, S. S., 33
Border, L.L.B., 83
Bosworth, K., 59
Boyer, E. L., 44
Brain, learning methods related to, 18–19
Bransford, J., 16
Braskamp, L. A., 47
Braxton, J. M., 80
Brinko, K. T., 33
Brown, A. L., 11, 14
Brown, J. S., 12, 13, 15, 16
Bruffee, K. A., 59
Bruner, J., 13, 15

California State University at Chico, 78–79
California Virtual University (CVU), 95
Campione, J., 14
Cannon, H. C., 62
Caring, by teachers, 62
Cashin, W. E., 31
Cate, F. H., 96
Cawyer, C. S., 64
Centra, J. A., 31, 41
Chance, P., 7
Chance statistics course, 71
Chi, J., 16
Chi, M., 9
Chickering, A. W., 45, 57, 76, 77, 79
Chism, N. V., 83, 84

Back Issue/Subscription Order Form

Copy or detach and send to:
Jossey-Bass Inc., Publishers, 350 Sansome Street, San Francisco CA 94104-1342

Call or fax toll free!
Phone 888-378-2537 6AM-5PM PST; Fax 800-605-2665

Back issues: Please send me the following issues at $23 each
(Important: please include series initials and issue number, such as TL90)

1. TL _____

_____

_____

$ _____ Total for single issues

$ _____ Shipping charges (for single issues *only;* subscriptions are exempt from shipping charges): Up to $30, add $5^{50} • $30^{01}–$50, add $6^{50} $50^{01}–$75, add $7^{50} • $75^{01}–$100, add $9 • $100^{01}–$150, add $10 Over $150, call for shipping charge

Subscriptions   Please ❑ start   ❑ renew my subscription to *New Directions for Teaching and Learning* for the year _____ at the following rate:

                ❑ Individual $58   ❑ Institutional $104
NOTE: Subscriptions are quarterly, and are for the calendar year only. Subscriptions begin with the spring issue of the year indicated above. For shipping outside the U.S., please add $25.

$ _____ Total single issues and subscriptions (CA, IN, NJ, NY and DC residents, add sales tax for single issues. NY and DC residents must include shipping charges when calculating sales tax. NY and Canadian residents only, add sales tax for subscriptions)

❑ Payment enclosed (U.S. check or money order only)

❑ VISA, MC, AmEx, Discover Card #_____ Exp. date_____

Signature _____ Day phone _____

❑ Bill me (U.S. institutional orders only. Purchase order required)

Purchase order #_____

Name _____

Address _____

_____

_____

Phone_____ E-mail _____

For more information about Jossey-Bass Publishers, visit our Web site at:
www.josseybass.com   **PRIORITY CODE = ND1**

Statement of Ownership, Management, and Circulation

1. Publication Title	2. Publication Number	3. Filing Date
NEW DIRECTIONS FOR TEACHING & LEARNING	0 2 7 1 – 0 6 3 3	10/1/99

4. Issue Frequency	5. Number of Issues Published Annually	6. Annual Subscription Price
QUARTERLY	4	$ 58 – indiv. $104 – inst.

7. Complete Mailing Address of Known Office of Publication *(Not printer)* *(Street, city, county, state, and ZIP+4)*
350 SANSOME STREET
SAN FRANCISCO, CA   94104
(SAN FRANCISCO COUNTY)

Contact Person
ROGER HUNT
Telephone
(415) 782-3232

8. Complete Mailing Address of Headquarters or General Business Office of Publisher *(Not printer)*

SAME AS ABOVE

9. Full Names and Complete Mailing Addresses of Publisher, Editor, and Managing Editor *(Do not leave blank)*

Publisher *(Name and complete mailing address)*
JOSSEY-BASS INC., PUBLISHERS
(ABOVE ADDRESS)

Editor *(Name and complete mailing address)* MARILLA D. SVINICKI
CTR FOR TEACHING EFFECTIVENESS/UNIV OF TX AT AUSTIN
MAIN BUILDING 2200
AUSTIN, TX   78712-1111

Managing Editor *(Name and complete mailing address)*
NONE

10. Owner *(Do not leave blank. If the publication is owned by a corporation, give the name and address of the corporation immediately followed by the names and addresses of all stockholders owning or holding 1 percent or more of the total amount of stock. If not owned by a corporation, give the names and addresses of the individual owners. If owned by a partnership or other unincorporated firm, give its name and address as well as those of each individual owner. If the publication is published by a nonprofit organization, give its name and address.)*

Full Name	Complete Mailing Address
JOHN WILEY & SONS INC.	605 THIRD AVENUE NEW YORK, NY 10158-0012

11. Known Bondholders, Mortgagees, and Other Security Holders Owning or Holding 1 Percent or More of Total Amount of Bonds, Mortgages, or Other Securities. If none, check box ▸ ☐ None

Full Name	Complete Mailing Address
SAME AS ABOVE	SAME AS ABOVE

12. Tax Status *(For completion by nonprofit organizations authorized to mail at nonprofit rates) (Check one)*
The purpose, function, and nonprofit status of this organization and the exempt status for federal income tax purposes:
☐ Has Not Changed During Preceding 12 Months
☐ Has Changed During Preceding 12 Months *(Publisher must submit explanation of change with this statement)*

PS Form **3526**, September 1998   *(See Instructions on Reverse)*

---

13. Publication Title	14. Issue Date for Circulation Data Below
NEW DIRECTIONS FOR TEACHING & LEARNING	SUMMER 1999

15.	Extent and Nature of Circulation		Average No. Copies Each Issue During Preceding 12 Months	No. Copies of Single Issue Published Nearest to Filing Date
a.	Total Number of Copies *(Net press run)*		1911	1756
b. Paid and/or Requested Circulation	(1)	Paid/Requested Outside-County Mail Subscriptions Stated on Form 3541. *(Include advertiser's proof and exchange copies)*	866	874
	(2)	Paid In-County Subscriptions *(Include advertiser's proof and exchange copies)*	0	0
	(3)	Sales Through Dealers and Carriers, Street Vendors, Counter Sales, and Other Non-USPS Paid Distribution	0	0
	(4)	Other Classes Mailed Through the USPS	0	0
c.	Total Paid and/or Requested Circulation *(Sum of 15b. (1), (2),(3),and (4))* ▸		866	874
d. Free Distribution by Mail *(Samples, complimentary, and other free)*	(1)	Outside-County as Stated on Form 3541		
	(2)	In-County as Stated on Form 3541		
	(3)	Other Classes Mailed Through the USPS	2	2
e.	Free Distribution Outside the Mail *(Carriers or other means)*		40	40
f.	Total Free Distribution *(Sum of 15d. and 15e.)* ▸		42	42
g.	Total Distribution *(Sum of 15c. and 15f)* ▸		908	916
h.	Copies not Distributed		1003	840
i.	Total *(Sum of 15g. and h.)* ▸		1911	1756
j.	Percent Paid and/or Requested Circulation *(15c. divided by 15g. times 100)*		95%	95%

16. Publication of Statement of Ownership
☒ Publication required. Will be printed in the WINTER 1999 issue of this publication.   ☐ Publication not required.

17. Signature and Title of Editor, Publisher, Business Manager, or Owner

Susan E. Lewis
SUSAN E. LEWIS
DIRECTOR OF PERIODICALS

Date
10/1/99

I certify that all information furnished on this form is true and complete. I understand that anyone who furnishes false or misleading information on this form or who omits material or information requested on the form may be subject to criminal sanctions (including fines and imprisonment) and/or civil sanctions (including civil penalties).

Instructions to Publishers

1. Complete and file one copy of this form with your postmaster annually on or before October 1. Keep a copy of the completed form for your records.

2. In cases where the stockholder or security holder is a trustee, include in items 10 and 11 the name of the person or corporation for whom the trustee is acting. Also include the names and addresses of individuals who are stockholders who own or hold 1 percent or more of the total amount of bonds, mortgages, or other securities of the publishing corporation. In item 11, if none, check the box. Use blank sheets if more space is required.

3. Be sure to furnish all circulation information called for in item 15. Free circulation must be shown in items 15d, e, and f.

4. Item 15h., Copies not Distributed, must include (1) newsstand copies originally stated on Form 3541, and returned to the publisher, (2) estimated returns from news agents, and (3), copies for office use, leftovers, spoiled, and all other copies not distributed.

5. If the publication had Periodicals authorization as a general or requester publication, this Statement of Ownership, Management, and Circulation must be published; it must be printed in any issue in October or, if the publication is not published during October, the first issue printed after October.

6. In item 16, indicate the date of the issue in which this Statement of Ownership will be published.

7. Item 17 must be signed.

Failure to file or publish a statement of ownership may lead to suspension of Periodicals authorization.

PS Form **3526**, September 1998 *(Reverse)*